Land of the Shapeshifter

Land of the Shapeshifter

by

Stephen W. F. Berwick

Parisburg Publishing
2011

Copyright © 2011 by Stephen W. F. Berwick
All rights reserved

Printed in the U.S.A.
October 2011 Printing

Stephen W.F. Berwick also has written:
Shapeshifter's Peace
In the Shadow of Agiocochook

Parisburg Publishing

parisburgpublishing.com
parisburg.com

ISBN-13:
978-1-61918-002-4

Acknowledgments

Heartfelt thanks to Stephen C. Shaw who encouraged me to write in order to free my spirit; Ngoc Quang Huynh who taught me to know my way home; Sukumar and Shanti Pattnaik, Tam Luu, Muoi Trieu, Keo Chanthasiri, Sasamoto Munetoshi, Goto Mieko and Valerie Laker who taught me that family isn't always through blood; Connie (Kim Won-suk) LaPlante who taught me that all cultures are one; S. David Siff whose patient confidence continues to inspire and guide me; Peter Brodeur, a true bonhomme whose stories about the Wôbanaki paint mind pictures that propel me to write; Susan McKevitt who guided me on the path back to my heritage; and, Sarah L. Browning who prodded me to write when I needed encouragement most.

Dedication

To my mother and father, Rosemary N. (Houle) and Nelson F. Berwick whose influence has guided my life.

Contents

Preface 9
    Abenaki Pronunciation *12*

Introduction 13
    Fighting Below Sugar Ball Bluff *13*
    Sayings For Moon Shifts *15*
    Ancient Wisdom for the People *19*
    Spaces of Good Medicine for the Heart *22*

The Stone People 25

The Profiles of Stone People 35

A Day at Concord 39

Mohawk Assault on the Penagok 49

The "First" to the Top of Agiocochook 65

Crows 75

A Petition for Land 87

The Rum Incident 97

Disillusion 105

Up in a Great Cloud of Fire 115

They Hang Medô-linô-winno-ak, Don't They? 127

Family History's Lessons 135
Abenaki-English Glossary 143
Native American Place Names in New England 150
About the Author 153

Preface

We as a people today move so quickly that we forget history's lessons. We forget what is in our blood waiting to teach us. Native Americans know who they are and where they came from. For many Native American peoples seven generations are important. In all things, great consideration is given to the connection between the living: the six generations before the living one and the six generations to come. To the Abenaki the dead are never really gone but are, as I have found in other cultures, always with us, the ancestral spirits are part of the environment and ready to assist their descendants. For my part, it is possible that I had not only English but may have also had Abenaki ancestors who lived at, or at the very least, visited Concord during the time that many of the following stories took place at the Place of the Falling Bank. I may also have Mohawk relatives who made the assault on the palisade at Penagok (Concord, "Place of the Falling Bank"). As such, partly out of respect, I have felt an overwhelming need to relate the stories of those who once dwelled here.

I am not a genealogist and make no pretense at being such; however, in researching my family's history I encountered information that links members of my family with Passaconaway, the Great Chief of the Penagok Confederation at the time of the Pilgrim's arrival at Patuxet. The information I found indicates family members had met with not only Passaconaway, but also his son, Waolinasad, and grandson, Kancamagus. There is also an early connection to Penagok, now Concord, going back to my 10th great-grandfather, Jonathan Danforth, as well as my now infamous 10th great uncle, Major Richard Waldron and my 10th great-grandmothers' nephews, Peter Coffin and Thomas Paine. Each of the men had met Passaconaway and Waolinasad while the Great Chiefs were at Penagok. Waldron, who had begun commerce with the Penagok by 1635, had been sent for by Passaconaway in 1659 while the Great Chief was at the Penagok fort. Then, as early as 1663, Waldron and Peter Coffin had a fur trading post at Penagok and Paine was at the post in 1668 when an Englishman named Dickinson was killed there by a Penagok over some dispute.

These and other disquieting facts came back to me as part of my family history. When I learned that my 10th great-grandfather, Captain Jonathan Danforth, brother to Deputy Governor Thomas Danforth, had been Massachusetts Bay Colony's chief land surveyor and had as a result carried out surveys that created lines/boundaries not recognized or understood by native peoples and later "a chief" or other native peoples deemed "an official" by the British, "acceded" to the new owner of land from my native ancestors, that I began to truly feel the pain of being on both sides deeply and personally. When I also learned that Jonathan Danforth was one of the two men who conducted the survey that granted Passaconaway land that should have been his anyway, it struck a chord. Since he had personally met Passaconaway, what did they think of each other? It was this same ancestor who in 1685 witnessed the land deed signed by Passaconaway's son, Waolinasad that "gave" Penagok to Jonathan Tyng. History generally acknowledges native peoples did not own land in the sense that British needed to "grant" or "sell" land to another. If the land deed was genuine, was Waolinasad aware of what he had done? These are perhaps questions whose answers can only be interpreted by extrapolation of evidence.

Perhaps some will say my view of history is skewed toward the Abenaki. As a descendant of both European and Native ancestors as well as a Buddhist-Animist, I try through my writing to be attuned to the ancestral voices in me. So far in the march of American history the European version of the story of what took place in what the Abenaki call "N'dakinna" and is today northern New England and southern Quebec, has long been heard; the Native voices have yet to be heard. It is my hope that stories will help long silenced voices to be heard.

Abenaki Pronunciation

Generally speaking, the consonants and vowels are similar to English but are spoken with less stress than English.

Aw   Sounds like "ow" in "now"

"8" or "ô."   Sounds like "aw" in "dawn"

Kw   Sounds like "Qu" in "Quiet"

W   Sounds like "Oo" at the beginning of a word

INTRODUCTION

Introduction

Fighting Below Sugar Ball Bluff

They fought below Sugar Ball,
    they died along Fort Eddy.
    They perished in the swamps,
    along the Morôdemak's sandy shore
    and on the autumn fields
    and could not be buried.
    Their flesh fed the crows.
    Even now when the wind is right
    long stilled voices talk to the hearts of those who walk
    amongst the moonlit pines:
    "Tell the crows,
    the messenger of the spirits,
    the gifter of corn,
    the giver of life,
    to tell the Great Spirit:
    "'They were surprised but were not afraid;

LAND OF THE SHAPESHIFTER

they died in the swamps,
along the Morôdemak's sandy shore
and on the autumn fields
and could not be buried.'"
"Tell the crows we could not escape them.
The invaders fought and we were both slain:
the spirits of the Mohawk continue to wander
as they cry for the lakes of their home."
Above the cornfields and river was once a palisade.
Was it north; was it south along the bluff?
You gathered the harvest but it was never eaten.
Who was there to pray for your spirits?
Do you still wander the swamps at night?
Do your will o'wisp spirits morph into I-393 headlights
as you nightly wander across your former battlefield?
You who fought to preserve your liberty and freedom,
though all would be in vain,
I think of you, Penagok,
your fight was not forgotten
for in the afternoon you went to battle
and at night you did not return.

(Adapted from an anonymous 1st century B.C. Chinese poem)

INTRODUCTION

NUMBER 1

Sayings For Moon Shifts
From The Time Before Time[1]

By Awassosem-Legwasiwinno[2]

PENAGOK:
WÔBANAKI
ALAMIKOS - THE GREETING MOON

When in the Greeting Moon's pale fire
The snow covers wigwam walls
You will know the fire greets you more
Than the gloom of your snowbound desire.

PIAÔDAGOS - BOUGH SHEDDING MOON

When snow begins bark to reveal
And from pine sap your nostrils begins to twitch and reel
Time to lace snow shoes and wake up your traps
Before the moon hibernates in the Moose hunter's lap.

---

[1] "Sayings for Moon Shifts" is based on 18th and early 19th century Farmer's Almanacs. Number 1 was the first edition.

[2] This is the author's Abenaki name, which means: "Bear that Dreams"

LAND OF THE SHAPESHIFTER

MOZOKAS - MOOSE HUNTING MOON

When the Hunting Moon is loose
Heed the antlers of the moose
For the maple is readying to flow
Like the ice freed Merrimack seeks the trail
Of day walker's strengthening glow.

SOGALIKAS - SUGAR MAKER MOON

The pulsing of wakened veins
Stirs the maple's golden blood to strain
Sweetening our sapped wintered lives
And the bees that begin to stir inside their hives.

KIKAS - FIELD PLANTING MOON

Beneath the pines and ancient palisade at Penakok
The time has arrived the three sisters to sow;
Beneath the corn maiden plant the squash to nourish the soil
And entwine sister bean around the stalk
So she on her skyward journey can walk.

NIKKSHIGAS - HOE TILLING MOON

Near the shore of Pemigewasset the fields spring awake
Sprouts and buds abound ready for the hoe the weeds to take;
Be careful in tilling not plants to spoil
Or else you may add insult to injury to grandmother's soil.

INTRODUCTION

TEMASKIKOS - BERRY RIPENING MOON

When green berries begin their shapes to shift
And red shows itself like a bursting gift
Ready and mend your birch bark containers and baskets of ash
For soon to overflowing they'll be for strawberries to stash.

TEMEZÔWAS - GATHERING MOON

The moon full over Winnipesaukee brings bounty to harvest
And though stinging things may grow buzzy and cocky
Free your smacking hand and ensure to gather vegetables
For you the barren winter moon to endure.

SKAMONKAS - CORN HARVEST MOON

When sunny fields along the Deep River pop and glow
Yellow, green, red, black and blue
You will feel the inner field
Turn deep inside of you.

PENIBAGOS - LEAF FALLING MOON

The three hunters have felled the sky bear
And its blood stains the mountains, branches and leaves
But despair not in the cave of your heart
For soon He Who Sleeps Through the Winter will shift his shape
And return above the starry trees.

Land of the Shapeshifter

MZATANOSKAS - FREEZING RIVER MOON

The sky bear has already climbed back above the starry trees
And the nasty stingy things have stilled their wings under frosty night walker's sway
And though every breath feels his moccasins frozen prints across your chest
Soon you'll forget the discomfort when ice fishing will be your favorite form of play.

PEBONKAS - WINTER MOON

When grandfather moon's fire has frozen above the Hidden One's face
One glowing eye will warm your heart when viewed within your wigwam's hearth;
But keep enough wood to ensure your hearth is as warm as your heart
When viewing the cold eye of the winter moon.

Introduction

Ancient Wisdom for the People

WHEN MOSQUITOES AND DEER FLIES COME A CALLING

When the air is steeped with steam
And the sky is filled with children's screams and stinging wings
Take and crush a sweet fern in your hand
Or wear a sprig of it in your hair band
Or give up battling the mosquitoes and deer flies all together
And pack the wigwam and seek the island in the middle of the stream
To sleep a cool night of stingless dreams.

SYRUPING MAPLE TIME

Day walker's descent;
Night walker's advent.
Boiled in darkness, maple tapped
Sweetens and mellows the sap.
As the moon is full
So is the syrup flavorful.

BEARING RED OCRE

When smearing your skin
with bear grease
and earth's blood ocre,
to escape the winter's cold
or the moon of stinging things,
in gratitude be
that red the land pulsates
shimmering life's force like rivers
to nourish our springs.

Land of the Shapeshifter

OF STONE ARROWS AND TOOLS

In the palm of your hand
Grasp a likely quartz, flint or other durable stone
Feel its grain by pressure of flesh and bone
Tap with your fingers to determine if its for chipping into a tool sound
Or good only for returning to the ground;
A stone arrow and tool is only as good as the rock
For in the heat of battle a warrior should rely on only a steady aim
Not an unnecessary cracked shock.

TOMAHAWK HEAD IN BOUNDARY STONE

When at peace atop the village boundary stone place a tomahawk
So that all will know your intents far and near;
For all who enter when in time of war
Remove the axe head for your intentions to be made clear.

GREAT STONE FACE

When in the midst of life chiseling you down
Consider the great stone face under the moon
And shift the arrow shape of your heart
Into a tree ringed and rooted evergreen to the ground.

Introduction

OAK TEA BROWNED

Immersed in a pond
Or drizzled from a bucket
Infuse your body
In oak leaf tea;
In staining the skin
From the burning day
You'll be pain free
And from insects
You won't be prey.
Newborns and babies
Should bathe in this brew
So that from sun's fever
And other stinging things
There'll be few.
The skin will be brown
Deflecting the sun
And in this way
One less combat
Will have to be won.

CORNING THE FIELDS

When white oak leaves
The size of a mouse's ear appears
And the first full moon upon sky nears
Then should women in fields by men cleared
Plant the corn for the new year.

Land of the Shapeshifter

Spaces of Good Medicine for the Heart

In the North -

GREAT STONE FACE

There is a place where no war or battle is allowed to progress
a sacred land where snows cover the ground for many circles of the moon
and only the pure hearted are allowed to trespass
and arrowheads have become a great profile of peace.

In Wind Eagle's land the Creator carved from living rock a face
for all who come beneath the mountain with serious intent, problems to arbitrate
the flaked profile was set with firm brow, chin, and nose
and an eye that pierces through clouded minds and hearts displaced

The visage is great medicine for all of pure intent to see;
Surrounded by the freshness of balsam, pine, white birch and maple
And frequented by the animal people who revere the sacred space
It is a welcome place to both the Mohawk and the children of the ash tree
And all who make no war but instead carve out from their stone imaginations hatred
Replacing it with hearts and minds that soar fresh, evergreen and free.

In the Center -

FOR THE STRONGHOLD OF THE HEART (PENAGOK)

At the crooked place where the sand moves the bank
And where the palisade looks upon the plain below
Have your canoe take the shape of a bow
And shoot for the place of vast fields of popping corn
For here is where shape shifters are reborn
Under Rough Mountain's shadowed stone
A new stronghold in the heart is sown.

(Penagok — present-day Concord, NH, was the stronghold of the
Penacook Indians, the name "Penakok" means "at the Falling Bank" and
has also has been translated as "At the Crooked Place." Both are apt as the likely
place of the fort was on a sandy bluff at the crook of the river
The weathering of the sandy banking was made by the meandering of the river.)

Introduction

AT THE RIVERS' FORK

Beskeodanak, near where the rivers "Swift" meets the "Land around the Waters"
Forking into the "Deep"
Is a village with origins deep-rooted in family tree lines
Standing beneath the hills in a glen of birch and pine.
Here above the lapping water at the tense bow
Visitors alight from canoes once spring melts the layered snow.
A boulder marks where the blunt nosed shad is in abundance,
Where mothers, fathers and offspring at the 3 rivers confluence
Into ancient relics have melted into the ground
That richly in ancestral lifeblood and marrow abounds.

PROFILE FALLS

From a deep hillside
To the Forked Village's north
Beside the Bemijijoasek along the Bear Grease Trail
A spring cascades forth.
Not far away water falls
Like Bemola, thundering down granite walls.
Camping a night here refreshes spirits and throats
Dampened under day walker's sweaty brow
The deep pool for weary muscles,
Offers shapes a shifting soak.

The Stone People

1

The Stone People

In Wind Eagle's land the Creator carved from living rock a face
for all who come beneath the granite cliff, troubles to arbitrate;
the flaked profile was set with a firm brow, chin, and nose
and an eye to pierce through clouded minds and hearts displaced.

This is sacred land where no war or battle is allowed to progress;
a holy site where deep snow swaddles the mountains for half the year;
where arrowheads made a grand profile of peace;
and where only pure hearts are permitted trespass.

The visage is great medicine for all of pure intent to see;
Surrounded by the freshness of balsam, spruce, white birch and maple
It is a welcome place to Mohawk and children of the ash tree
And all who make no war but carve out hatred from their stone heads
Replacing it with hearts and minds that soar fresh, evergreen and ever free.

"There, up in the clouds, do you see?" the Medôlinôwinno Toothless Bear asked his grandson, Little Tree. Toothless Bear was so named because in form and aspect he was powerful like a bear and had always been peaceful by nature, fighting only when necessary. He also had many teeth missing due to his advanced age - some said he had already seen 80 winters - much less than the Penacook Chief Babiwseso-Ogawinno (Passaconaway) for sure but still a venerable age. Toothless Bear was a great friend of the Penacook chief who himself was a onetime warrior who had fought many in battle, but after hearing the Great Spirit's words to walk the path of peace was now dedicated to that path.

"Where?" Little Tree asked.

Land of the Shapeshifter

"Up higher. Up there where the falcon rides the wind" Toothless Bear responded, gesturing with his chin to the place where the Great Stone Face hung on a steep cliff side far above the clear water pond and just below a bank of fluffy clouds that resembled milkweed floss. At the very edge of the clouds could be seen the sliver of a diaphanous moon.

"I see him!" Little Tree exclaimed in awe at the sight. It was a sight to behold. It was a sight that had been beheld for generation upon generation by Penagok, Bemijijoasek, Mohawk, Huron and many others traveling through the notch from north to south. The pond was a place to rest and a place to reflect.

Toothless Bear was Medôlinôwinno, "a Person of Medicine." He had brought his grandson to the White Mountains to introduce him to a powerful spirit. The Nwaskw - "spirit" - of the Great Stone Face.

"He's a stone person. A-se-ni-ki-wa-kw. Do you remember how I told you they were made by Gluskab?"

"Yes" replied Little Tree as he continued gaping above the pond, his eyes and mouth following the firm brow, chin and nose and the eye that he sensed could see everything everywhere at any and every time.

Toothless Bear waited for his grandson to speak but soon realized he was absorbed in the scene.

"Tell me what you know," Toothless Bear said to his grandson.

Little Tree recited the tale:

"Gluskab was walking around the land one day after he made legs for himself and realized he was lonely. In his loneliness he de-

The Stone People

cided to create people. So he made the stone giants called Asenikiwakw. The fire in their eyes was the flint. It is the same spirit in the stone that we use to create fire."

"Yes, good." his grandfather said.

"Now as I told you before the Great Creator had gone to sleep. In his loneliness the Great Creator dreamed and tears began falling from his eyes. Those tears hit the fire in the stone which made lightning. The lightning made steam. From that steam came life. As the Great Creator dreamed he saw his creation. Suddenly he heard a voice. The Great Creator looked to see where the voice came from. It was from Odzihozo 'The One who makes Himself from Something' who came to be from the dust that fell from the Great Creator's hands.

'Here I am,' said Odzihozo.

'Who are you?' asked the Great Creator.

'I sprang from the dust that fell from your hands' came the answer.'"

Little Tree added:

"And the mountains, rivers and lakes were created by Odzihozo when he dragged his body around."

"Yes" Toothless Bear responded.

Little Tree continued:

"When he realized he had forgotten to make legs, Odzihozo made a pair so that he could stand. Upon standing he became Gluskab."

Land of the Shapeshifter

"Good. Now back to the stone giants."

Little Tree began:

"Gluskab soon found that the hearts of the stone giants were hard and cold so he destroyed them."

"Yes. Do you know why?"

"Yes. Wherever these stone giants went they stomped and romped and destroyed the land and trees. After they were destroyed their bones became the rocks that cover the land. Some of the stone giants escaped. Gluskab let them go. Gluskab then took an arrow and shot his medicine arrows into the brown, yellow, black, red and white ash trees. The trees became people. The brown ash became the Abenaki – Alnôbak which means the "People." From the bark came the little people, bokwjimen, who are keepers of the summer."

"Excellent! You remembered well," his grandfather said, smiling.

"Now as your tale said, some escaped."

"Yes. But where did they go?" asked Little Tree.

"Look around you. But most of all look above you."

Little Tree looked around and then above him.

"The Great Stone Face was one of those who escaped?"

Toothless Bear answered:

"Yes. You see throughout these mountains you can find many faces of the stone people, but this is one of the most powerful. He

The Stone People

is like the others. All are 'Nwaskw' - 'spirit.' But this spirit is special. As you already found out, his profile is like that of a great chief. He was a leader."

"Leader of the stone people?"

"Perhaps."

"And also because this place where he resides is so beautiful?"

Toothless Bear smiled.

"Yes. Because the Great Stone Face hangs out above the lake which is clear as mica and reflects all that is in our mind," Toothless Bear explained to his grandson. "Water and rocks abound here – water and rocks that connect us to the spirits."

"Is that why we connect hills and ponds with low stone rows so that they are shown as consecrated?" asked Little Tree.

"Yes. To show them as places of spirit."

Sunbeams came and went as shadows shifted above the mountain peaks. Toothless Bear gestured toward the high peaks rising like a forest and rock palisade across from the Great Stone Face.

"This whole place is special. It is a sacred place. Not just the Great Stone Face but these mountains. Above us, on the high peaks is where the thunder spirits live. Their place is very hard to reach. You must climb and climb and the way is very rugged with boulders and slippery rocks every place. It is also very steep. I once climbed the third peak up to where the trees grow runty to obtain a vision, but did not go any further so that I wouldn't disturb the spirits living atop the peaks," Toothless Bear said to his grandson.

While what he said was true, it was also true that the higher he climbed the steeper the grade became making his leg muscles ache. Besides, what was the point to climbing to the top? The good firewood and herbs were below. Why anger the spirits just to see if they were there or not?

Toothless Bear continued:

"I saw along the slopes beautiful falling water that comes from far above the trees. I was young and adventurous and was tempted to find the source of that water, but, as I said, I dared climb no higher. Through the trees I saw a great clearing where there were no trees or soil. It was a sacred space. It was a place of spirits. You can see it up there on the third peak, not far from the top. It shines under the sunlight. But, as I said, the thunder spirits change the weather up there on a whim. It is dangerous to be there when they change the weather."

Little Tree placed his hand above his eyes and squinted at the clearing high on the mountain that shone like flecks of mica under the flickering sunlight. His eyes followed the ridgeline, noticing how each peak was heaped up high like the clam shell mounds that he saw at the beaches along the sea where he went with his band during the summer.

"Near here, from the clearing where trees have fallen, you can see another face. That spirit may have at one time been a warrior who did lookout to ensure no one invaded his people's land."

He noticed Little Tree trying to locate the other stone face. Toothless Bear laughed.

"You can not see him from here, grandson. It is easy to miss since it is smaller and the face is downcast. Now, just as the stone people once lived and were shape shifted into spirits when they were destroyed so will we all die one day and shape shift into spirit. The same is true for the Great Stone Face."

"Do you mean someday he will disappear, too?"

"Yes. All things have a beginning and an end. Some day he will join the others" said Toothless Bear.

"Does the Great Creator continue to sleep?"

"Yes. He is asleep. When he awakens all that exists will disappear."

"All life is only a dream," said Little Tree.

"Yes. Life is only a dream. It is only in dreams that we really live. That is why we pay close attention to dreams. In dreams we are in touch with the Great Creator."

A breeze blew gently across the pond bringing with it the pungent scent of spruce and balsam and the screech of a blue jay.

"Now when we look upon the Great Stone Face we should ponder on who the stone giants once were and what happened to them. We should look into the pond and see the image in the pond that disappears as soon as a pebble is thrown into it. The ripples are like moments in our life that gradually disappear."

"But why is this place so special?"

"It is so special because it is a place to see one of the first ones. It is a place of reflection. It is a place where we can look into ourselves. As persons of medicine we must do this so that we can help heal others. Do you see his face?"

"Yes" responded Little Tree.

"Well, it is made of much the same stone as that which has been used for generations upon generations to make tools and weapons. There is quartz and granite there on that mountain. We use granite for many things like tomahawks and arrow shaft straighteners; the quartz for arrows to create weapons to kill or to get meat. But the same stone can be used in another way. It can be used for pecking stones, pestles and mortars to grind corn meal, amulets for protection, or attached to sticks so that we can poke holes in the ground for seeds to be sown."

Standing Bear looked at the mountain and said:

"So, when we look up at the Great Stone Face we can realize that if we have hearts that are too hard and cold like those of the stone giants then we too may be destroyed."

"Yes."

"Like in anger?"

"Yes, like when we are angry or want to destroy instead of walking the path of peace."

"Then we should not set our minds in granite, instead they should be free like the water."

"Yes. We should be able to absorb the ripples that upset the quietness of our life. And like the pond, we should nourish our bodies and spirits and reflect on our thoughts to make sure we are not stone headed and immovable."

The Stone People

Toothless Bear and Little Tree looked up at the Great Stone Face. It was a breathtaking sight. A reminder of life. Of the permanency of impermanence.

Land of the Shapeshifter

2

The Profiles of Stone People

Long, long, long ago. Long before Agiocochook took its final shape. Long before the great storm spirit Maji Nwaskw came to dwell atop Agiocochook's summit. Long before the crow brought corn to the Land of the Merrimack River there lived a people known to the Abenaki as Se-ni-ki-wa-kw, the "Stone People." The Stone People were the first people and had been made by Nawawas, "the One Who Comes to Us" whose name also means "the Creator," so that they would keep him company.

Among the Stone People were two brothers. One brother was gentle and kind and lived at peace with all the Stone People as well as the animals that dwelled on the land. His name was Looks Far. The other brother, Looks Near, was stubborn, hard headed but strong of features and strength. Looks Near was also very argumentative and took great enjoyment in creating discord among the Stone People. He was also intensely vain and often gazed into the surface of water to see his image reflected back at him.

One day while the brothers were out walking along the trail that leads through what we now know as Franconia Notch, the brothers came upon a beautiful woman named Mist-on-the-Mountain who was swimming in a pond beneath a granite ledge. Mist-on-the-Mountain had heretofore been unknown to the brothers who lived alone in an isolated ravine. But to the other stone people she was legendary. So was her wicked nature. Like the granite Mist-on-the-Mountain was hard hearted and took pleasure in the effect that her beauty had on others. She took particular delight in creating

35

LAND OF THE SHAPESHIFTER

dissension. She like all the stone people knew the brothers were close to each other and she felt jealousy for their happiness.

"I've no one who cares about me," she thought to herself. "Why should they alone be so happy?"

As Looks Far and Looks Near came near the pond Mist-on-the-Mountain glanced sultrily at Looks Far. With just that one gaze Mist-on-the-Mountain made Looks Far fall madly in love with her. She then threw her glance upon Looks Near who also fell in love with her.

Now ever since childhood there had been friendly rivalry between the two brothers Looks Far and Looks Near. They were always challenging each other. Up to that point it had kept them entertained. If Looks Far shot an arrow and hit a target 100 yards away, Looks Near would have to better him, shooting an arrow and hitting a target 101 yards away. And so it went. So although Looks Near was uninterested in Mist-on-the-Mountain, he felt the need to have her love as to do so would be a challenge to Looks Near. Unfortunately, as the subsequent history of the ash tree peoples will show, there is no greater cause for fighting than to secure the love of another. Looks Far became enraged with jealousy. Without warning Looks Far struck Looks Near. Looks Near struck back. The ensuing battle lasted seven days and seven nights. As they battled they destroyed everything in their wake. In the end, Looks Far killed Looks Near.

At this time the Creator, who had been away visiting the Great Bear who lives among the stars, felt something was wrong. When the Creator returned to earth he found that the land was devastated and all the Stone People and animals, except for Looks Far and Mist-on-the-Mountain were dead. The Creator became angry and with one look destroyed both Looks Far and Mist-on-the-Mountain. In his sadness the Creator decided to create people

The Profiles of Stone People

again, but this time instead of making people from stone he determined to make them from the ash tree.

"Stone people have stone hearts and care nothing about anyone but themselves. The ash tree is green and its heart grows as it grows. The wood will make good people."

With that the Creator created white people from white ash; red people from red ash; black people from black ash; and, yellow people from yellow ash. The Creator then decided to make examples of Looks Near, Looks Far and Mist-on-the-Mountain so that the ash tree people would learn from their lesson. He placed the profile of Looks Near in the notch above the lake where Looks Near often admired at his profile. He placed Mist-on-the-Mountain near Looks Near but far enough away that they could not see each other. Mist-on-the-Mountain was placed so that she gazes only at a nearby Cliffside, away from Looks Near. Today, if you look toward Eagle Cliff you can see her. She is the Watcher. Looks Far he placed south of the notch so that he gazes off toward the land where the red ash people live. Today we see him as Indian Head.

In 2002, taking pity on Looks Near who had wept for thousands of winters at not being able to see Mist-on-the-Mountain nor his profile over a thousand feet above the lake, the Creator made a mist that moved the stones that held up Looks Near's profile. The stones slipped and with it Looks Near crashed back to earth and his spirit was released.

Though few people are aware of them today, the Stone People are still here, all around us. They are our ancestors, our Grandmothers and Grandfathers. The original people. When we go to sweat lodges they give us counsel.

Land of the Shapeshifter

3

A Day at Concord

(1565 C.E.)

Call me Babiwseso-Ogawinno. My name means "Very-Little-One-of-He-Who-Likes-to-Sleep-So-Well." The English who settled this land called me "Child of the Bear" and shortened my name to Passaconaway. But that's another story.

Shortly after I was born my people faced a great sickness that took many lives. Then, just before the Great Dying Time that took place across the Dawnland, the Great Chief Bashaba who headed an alliance to the east of us along the seacoast from Pemaquid down to Nahant became involved in a bitter rivalry with the Mi'kmaq over fur trading rights with the French. In the ensuing conflict Bashaba was killed by the Mi'kmaq. The Mi'kmaq then raided southward across the Dawnland into the land of the Wampanoag, bringing back with them sicknesses left by the strangers. The sicknesses killed more than half of my people over the course of several winters. We refer to this as the Great Dying Time. On the heels of the Great Dying Time came the Maneaters who you call Mohawk. The Maneaters attacked us at Penagok, killing more than 350 warriors and as many women and children. It was during the winter moon following the Great Dying Time and the attack by the Mohawk, that the strangers from across the sea came to live at the Patuxet village where nearly everyone had died from sickness.

But I want to speak of the time before death came to live in my land. A time of happiness. It's funny how once everyday occurrences become your most important and happiest memories.

Land of the Shapeshifter

Everyday occurrences become the things that you cling to in order to retain a link to your past. A link to the way it was before your world was turned upside down. A link to how things are "supposed to be" but are no longer.

I remember one such day. I was a boy. It was a day when nothing much happened. A day that will live with me until I go to meet my ancestors in the above land. Listen to my story of an average day at Penagok which you now call Concord, New Hampshire in the time before death and the white man came to live in this land.

The deer hide flap had been pushed aside and the warmth from Day Traveler reached inside the wigwam's mat covered bark walls. I lay for a while atop the sleeping platform. I can still feel the soft fur against my back and legs. I rolled to my side and lowered my head to look outside. Looking out the opening you could see fields stretching along both banks of the river as far as your eye could see. As the corn reached maturity you could see two waving rivers of corn stalks lining both sides of the Morôdemak River, paling the blue water in comparison to the cornstalk's brilliant sunlit green.

I can see my mother's face, her eyes squinting in the smoke as she smiled up at me through the dim light:

"You are awake! We thought you were hibernating!," my mother teased.

"He sniffed out the food just like a bear," my grandmother laughingly added as I rubbed the stinging remainder of sleep away from my eyes.

"Your father has just gone out to check the tobacco plantings," my mother, smiling, said to me.

I got up and stretched.

A Day at Concord

"Later he'll meet with the council to decide when to go to Namaskik" added my mother.

Visions of the great falls at Namaskik as well as the annual salmon run at the weirs below the falls cascaded in my mind as I thought of going there.

My mother grinned:

"... and also to decide on the day to leave for Zobagw."

I was excited! The word "Zo-ba-goh" was our word for the sea.

"I thought that'd wake you up," my grandmother said, laughing at me, as she stirred dying embers to life.

The thought of the salt laden air invigorated my mind. You notice immediately a change in the air when you arrive at the dunes. During the hot and heady humid summer that settled in the valley of the Morôdemak you would not want to stay at Penacook and swelter when you could be feasting on clambakes at the sea. The same for us. Many of our village would move to the sea after planting the corn to escape and enjoy the bounty of lobster, clams, crabs and fish. You cannot imagine the sweetness of clams and fish roasted slowly under seaweed. Your mouth salivates and your tongue dances in anticipation.

"What do you want to eat when you get there?" my mother asked.

"Lobster!," I said, without hesitation.

"Lobster!" my sister, Smiling-on-Water, readily agreed.

Land of the Shapeshifter

My mother and grandmother shook their heads, smiling at our ready responses.

"Always lobster," my grandmother said wryly.

"I prefer clams," she said, her eyes drooling as she thought of them.

"Yes. Clams. The bellies melt on your tongue like fat. There is nothing quite as good," she sighed.

My mother looked at her mother with affection.

"Clams are delicious," my mother said, stirring the stew.

"Ah," my grandmother exhaled, "But I won't be going. It's too far for me to go now. Your grandfather and I will stay here this season."

"I want you to come," I said quickly.

"It won't be the same without you there," my sister agreed.

My grandmother looked at my mother and then over at me and my sister.

"There will come a time when you'll have to do things without us, grandson. You'll have to do things on your own," she said, patting some ground corn meal, dried berries, water and bear grease into little cakes that she wrapped in a leaf and baked in hot ashes.

"What are you going to do today," my mother asked as she handed me an already cooked corn cake.

A Day at Concord

"I am going fishing with Stinks-Like-a-Skunk," I said, nibbling a bit of the cake with my right hand while scratching my eyes with my left.

Stinks-Like-a-Skunk had received his name because he had been sprayed by a skunk. He hoped to someday outgrow that name. He did but died in battle with the Maneaters.

"Be careful near the brook. The-One-who-Rattles was seen there yesterday," my grandmother warned.

"Ahuh."

My little sister, always quiet and smiling, asked if she could go.

"I want to go," Smiling-on-Water said to my mother.

My grandmother stroked my sister's long black hair.

"I need you to help me this morning to finish the plantings," my mother told Smiling-on-Water through smiling teeth.

My sister pouted.

"We have to finish before we leave for Zobagw," my mother explained.

My sister smiled.

"Okay," my sister replied, sad that she couldn't go with me, but as excited as I was to be going to the sea.

My grandmother shook her head, laughing at herself how easily Smiling-on-Water gave in after being reminded of Zobagw.

Land of the Shapeshifter

"I was like you, too," she said to my sister Smiling-on-Water.

I took the cake and headed off to find my friend.

All along the Morôdemak River you would find villagers were waking up in their wigwams. Soon backs would be bending under the tepid sun, men planting odamô (tobacco) and women planting corn in mounds up and down the flat land along the river during the next moon, and the moon after more corn would be planted.

In the corn mound a fish, sometimes near the seacoast people used chopped horseshoe crabs, was inserted for fertilizer. Four kernels of corn to a hill were planted, as well as four kidney beans and squash. Women broke the ground with roughly flaked stone tools shaped like a pointing finger attached to long poles. Seeds were poked into the ground. Beans were planted in the same mound as corn so the bean could climb the corn. Around the corn was planted squash. The squash gave energy to the soil and helped the other plants. One of my favorite treats was to suck the sweet juice from the green corn stalks.

At our village lived about one hundred people, more or less, depending upon the season. Just outside the village was a tree where we tied the skulls of animals who had given their lives to feed our spirits. The bones were left to show our respect to the animals. Nearby was our burying ground. In our way, those who had gone to Wlinadialibna – the Happy Hunting Grounds - had already become Nwaskw - a spirit. The Great Creator was never seen, but communicated through Nwaskw. Nwaskw were always present, their bond everlasting. As such, we treated our dead ancestors with respect. The dead had immortal souls. If people lived good lives they could go to Wlinadialibna when they died. If they had not lived good lives and were thieves, murderers and liars they were doomed to wander after they died. The dead, their legs flexed to the stomach and hands before the face, were wrapped in mats and furs. Graves were dug shallow and lined with branches and leaves. The deceased was put into the pit with their head facing east. Depending on the family, tools, food and weapons as well as pendants were buried with them. Death released the spirit to the land where there was no sorrow. The deceased was sometimes buried with red hematite that we called "olaman." In our belief, the red nuggets were like blood and as such the olaman were believed to give energy and life to the deceased.

On the opposite side of the Morôdemak, your eyes would pierce the mist rising above the water to see the palisade floating like a cloud above the sandy bluffs and see tall straight white pines, fat red pines and squat jack pines called "strange red pine - bilowi basaakw" melting into the sunlight. Your eyes would spy an eagle spanning its wings, floating on the wind, as he scanned for his evening meal. Your eyes would feast on the peace of the scene, filling your heart with happiness. Such was how I felt as a boy.

I met up with my friend Stinks-Like-A-Skunk.

"Didn't put enough bear grease on this morning," I said to Stinks-Like-a-Skunk as he smacked a mosquito.

"I did. They are just hungry," he said, reaching into a thicket of sweet fern to pull a spray to wear in his headband.

"Let's go to the brook," I suggested, taking a trail that lead to a small river that drains into the Morôdemak.

Day after day throughout the moon of Kikas followed as the one before. Awakening, eating, meeting Stinks-Like-a-Skunk, taking the trail to the brook. The trail was always kept clear of underbrush. Even the forests were cleared by burning the brush twice a year. Land was also cleared by girdling the trunks then setting fire at the base of the trees. The charred tree could then be easily felled

Land of the Shapeshifter

by an ax. In the woods around Penagok, where trails led in all directions, you would find the forest ground was cleared of brush, weeds and poison ivy, allowing fruit bearing bushes, birches, pines, beeches, oaks and other varieties of nut bearing trees to rise to the sky. It was important to keep the forest floor clean so that, among other things, the nolkak (deer) would thrive and thereby provide meat to the hunters.

"Shh... Listen. Do you hear?," Stinks-Like-a-Skunk asked me.

"Hear what?"

Our ears listened.

"Thunderbirds" Stinks-Like-a-Skunk responded

"Badôgiak?" I asked him. Badôgiak is the Abenaki word for thunderbird.

"They're flying up to the mountains," Stinks-Like-a-Skunk responded.

Stinks-Like-a-Skunk was right. In the distance we could see their eyes flashing. On their backs were lakes that they shook off as rain.

"They are far off and won't come this way," I said as we headed into the woods.

The woods you would find thrived with sound during the late spring, summer and early autumn. The sounds of activity would fill you with appreciation for all life. Along the trails during the summer the arms and fingers of trees drooped heavily under Day Traveler's advance across the sky, the shoulders of many chirping with the songs of birds calling to each other while leaves rustled from the movement of a thousand tiny scampering feet. In the beaver ponds you would find moose wallowing in the water, crunching vegetation while the sagging scraggly branches of immature pôbnôdageso (tamaracks) stretched and creaked as they dipped their feathery fingers lazily in the water like a maiden flirting with a young warrior.

Day Traveler had walked six fingers across the sky when Stinks-Like-A-Skunk and I returned to the village with several trout. My mother shared them with others, and they in turn gave us some deer meat. That night the sunset was brilliant. The Morôdemak blushed like ochre used in graves, followed by fire. When dusk came my grandfather remarked:

"A sunset like that is a beautiful sight. It is nwaskw and filled with power. But it's this power that can become a sunrise of blood. Before you were born," grandfather began, "Day Traveler also ended his journey with bright color just like this such a night. The next day we learned that it had been a warning of danger - we were attacked by the Maneaters."

In those days the Mohawk did hit and runs.

My grandmother said: "They hadn't warned us of their attack. They came like thieves. Your grandfather can not look at a sunset without remembering how your uncle was killed," my grandmother added.

"He had been killed by a Mohawk," my grandfather added.

They both became sullen at the thought.

These images were long ago pecked into my mind and serve as a marker indicating direction to the best memories that strengthen me. Whenever I am lonely or overcome by the horror of death around me and feel powerless, the peaceful images of my youth rise above the inundation that threatens to flood and destroy everything around me. The memories remind me of how sweet life can be and to focus on giving the young Penagok a chance for a happy life. In that way, I can go on amidst the ever changing current of life.

But other images float across the surface of the sky. Change comes to your life when you least expect it. So to it came to the Penagok. The Great Dying Time came when we were least ready for it. It was as if Maji Nwaskw, the "Bad Spirit," that dwells atop the bone white peak of Gôdag Wajo (known as Mt. Washington) had covered Day Traveler, plunging the land into blackness.

4

Mohawk Assault on the Penagok

(c. 1616 C.E)

Unlike their human counterparts, bear people councils are light hearted and the shape of it shifts with the story told. Sharp and witty, bears love a good story. Among the bear people who hold Sky Council are five who stand out among the rest - they are Fire Eyes, Scorching Tail, Gray Ear, Great Heart and Matted Fur.

Fire Eyes, like all Bear People on the Sky Council, is wise and compassionate. Fire Eyes got his name from the intensity and seriousness of his flaring gaze when he related stories. It's said that through his eyes you could see down to the fire that animated him. Fire Eyes, the Chief of the Bear People who hold sky council, receives his authority from consensus and respect of the others.

In addition to Fire Eyes there is also Scorching Tail who got his name because he sits too close to the council fire where he singes his stubby tail. Scorching Tail, a deep thinker, is noted for his undiluted sarcasm and ready wit.

Then there is Gray Ear, whose analytical skills were called upon by the others in reaching consensus on important decisions. He received his name due to the two gray smudges just below his ears.

Great Heart, whose pupils seemed always to be swimming, was a bear whose heart ached at the suffering humans created for themselves and each other. She was also younger and more inquisitive than the others.

The last of the five was Matted Fur who rarely spoke but who, although unkempt, was greatly respected for his intelligence and keen scent of the situation.

"Listen as the Great Chief of the Penagok Confederacy, Passaconaway, whose Abenaki name 'Babiwseso-Ogawinno' means 'the-Very-Little-One-of-He-Who-Likes-to-Sleep-So-Well' tells the story of the Mohawk assault on the Penagok," Fire Eyes said. "In less poetic language he is known as 'Child-of-the-Bear.'"

"Passaconaway will tell you about the great battle that took place at the Penagok palisade atop Sugar Ball Bluff. The Leaf Falling Moon had entered the land of the Penagok located in the center of Wôbanaki - the Dawnland. By the 19th century the land that was formally the Dawnland had become a part of southern Quebec, New Hampshire, Vermont, Maine and northern Massachusetts. Soon the leaves would be stained with the Great Bear's blood. The Abenaki word 'Magua' meaning 'Maneater' and which the Penagok used to refer to the Mohawks, filled the woods and mountains of the Dawnland with dread and terror," Fire Eyes said, inner fire reflecting the council flames in front of him.

"How did the Mohawk come to be called 'Magua?,'" Great Heart asked.

"Propaganda that was partly perpetuated by the Mohawk themselves. Remember, terror is one way of winning an otherwise stalemate. Human history is filled with wars won through propaganda. The overblown claims about the Magua were pregnant with hints and suppositions that gestated more far-fetched claims that had nothing to do with reality so that when the Mohawk strike against one of their enemies finally came the terror that was given

Mohawk Assault on the Penagok

birth was far worse than the actual attack itself. It was a type of psychological warfare. Among the wild claims about the Mohawk that circulated among the wigwams of the Dawnlanders were claims that at the first hearing of the Mohawk war cry 'Hadree! Hadree! Sucomee! Sucomee! - We come! We come! To suck your blood! To suck your blood!' the enemies of the Mohawk would be struck with such vivid terror that they would, if close to a precipice, dash themselves against the rocks far below in order to die instantly instead of waiting to be devoured by the man-eaters. It wasn't true, of course, but such stories have a way of validating themselves without proof. A rumor can become a truth when it isn't checked by reality. You see, if their enemies had compared their Mohawk experiences with each other they would have discovered the Mohawk to be less inclined to blood letting than the claims that haunted the landscape. But, the very fact that the reports of the Mohawk blood thirst existed caused them to be perpetuated into superstitious internal terror that lived in the minds of the Dawnlanders," Fire Eyes explained.

"Did all the Dawnlanders have this visceral fear of the Mohawk," asked Great Heart.

"No. Although the Penagok heard the same claims and were unsure of their authenticity, the Penagok would not give in to the Mohawks. They refused to be overawed and paralyzed with terror by the rumors of the belligerent Mohawk. So, they resisted and fought back hard."

"Weren't the Mohawk surprised by the Penagok resistance?" asked Great Heart.

"It irked and no doubt amazed the Mohawk that the Penagok were resilient and would retaliate with as much ferocity as they'd received," Fire Eyes said.

Land of the Shapeshifter

"Why did they keep harassing the Penagok?" Great Heart questioned.

"It was partly the challenge and partly because they believed they would win even when the evidence was that they wouldn't. They'd met their match in the Penagok."

"What was the Penagok warrior's thoughts about fighting the Mohawk?" asked Scorching Tail.

"As in all humanity there are those who even in the face of superstition and reports of blood thirst were eager to fight and show their own mettle. The Penagok were such a one as these. Under the leadership of Passaconaway, the Penagok believed they themselves were invincible against their enemies. As war chief before the founding of the Pine Tree Confederation that united all the tribes of New Hampshire under the leadership of Passaconaway, he fought like a bear crazed by the smell of blood!"

"No crazy bears here," Scorching Tail commented.

"Present company excluded," Fire Eyes agreed.

"However, we know how we all can get, especially a mother with cubs. Well, Passaconaway was like that. He fought against the Mohawk with all his might. Let's hear his recitation of it."

Planets revolved inside the Great Bear constellation as Passaconaway related his tale:

For a long time the Mohawk had scouted us to discover our weaknesses. They were like ghosts hiding among trees, watching our every move. We felt their presence but when we searched for them, they disappeared into the trees. Imagine the sensation of knowing someone is watching your every move; watching you eat,

Mohawk Assault on the Penagok

sleep, drink, make love... all the while just waiting for a chance to kill you all because they can. You can't do anything. You search for them, but they aren't there. Yet, you know they are there, just beyond your reach. That's how life was just before they attacked.

As our people died the Mohawk came to take advantage of our situation. The Mohawk were part of the Iroquois Long House Federation. The Iroquois, the story tellers told us, had moved into Algonquin lands long ago from the south, pushing us from our lands. The speech and ways of these Magua as well as others of the five nations that are part of the Iroquois Long House Federation were different from us. Whenever a chance arose for them to harass us, they did so. Such a chance happened after the Great Dying Time when more than half of our people died from unknown disease brought by people from across the Great Water. If we had not been reduced by disease that ravaged the land the Magua would not have been able to engage us in battle.

We knew the Magua and they knew and feared us. We could hold our own against them, and for as long as any one can remember, had responded to every attack against us by an equal measured response. If they killed one of us out of revenge, we, eventually would do the same to them and the circle would go on and on. Not one of us would allow them to shame us or to capture us. We knew they would take us back to their village where we'd be insulted then beaten, forced to run naked through a gauntlet. If a captive survived they might be adopted into a family but the chance was slim. We knew that if we were captured we wouldn't be adopted into their tribe like we did to those whom we gave mercy. We knew that if we were captured we would die a long, slow lingering death. As we slowly died the pain would be great and we, in our pride, would not cry out. We would be taunted as we sang our death song while they tortured us to death. It was believed by us that they would eat bits of us to absorb our spirits.

Land of the Shapeshifter

They wanted our spirits to enhance theirs. We refused to give it to them. We looked to the clouds and let our spirits go there.

It was widely believed by the Penagok that the Mohawk resorted to cannibalism when there was no food around or to steal the spirits of those they killed. That is why we called them Magua meaning "man eaters."

"Ah, the propaganda you mentioned," Great Heart said.

"Yes. And, very effective."

"How did the Mohawk feel about being called Maneaters?," asked Great Heart.

"Of course, the Mohawk didn't relish being thought of as maneaters, but it was useful."

As a Penagok you were always ready for death. Death for us was a part of life; life a part of death. Neither existed. Only in dreams is anything real.

"Death is to be faced calmly," my grandfather told me. "To cry out in pain is to shame not only yourself but the seven generations before you and after you. Death, grandson, is to be calmly accepted and to be quietly endured in your heart as the enemy torments your flesh. You must eat the bitterness. Calm your spirit. Be reflective. The stronger you are, the more deep is your pride in your freedom of spirit. No matter how you are tortured, you are to rise above it, your spirit like an eagle rising and soaring above the pain. As death comes to you and enters your body, you sing your song of triumph, asking the ancestors and Nwaskw, your spirit protector, to bear witness to your victory over your enemy. Your victory over your fears."

Mohawk Assault on the Penagok

Even at the young age of no more than five winters I understood what my grandfather was telling me. He was telling me a fact of life. There was no doubt in my mind even then what was required of me and of what I had to require of myself. We weren't people without feelings. Your heart felt everything. Your eyes saw everything. But you couldn't get lost with the feelings. Feelings destroyed.

The Magua were cruel, yes. It is true. But they were really doing nothing any different than what the rest of us were doing. We, too, did the same to enemies. It was a way of soothing the spirits of the warriors who had died in fighting the enemies. Those not chosen to die were adopted into our families to replace those who had been killed by the enemy.

The difference between us Penagok and the Magua was that we did not eat our enemies. But to act with ferocity toward your enemy was to be expected. It was a way to ensure security and that no one laid claim to your hunting and fishing places. We learned it from the bears.

"Us?" asked Great Heart.

"Seems so," answered Scorching Tail.

"Yes. From bears," came Fire Eyes' response.

"Observation of our human planed brethren," Fire Eyes extrapolated. The others understood.

"Life can be cruel in that plane," sighed Great Heart.

"For the humans if they were treated with respect and asked beforehand to be allowed to fish, hunt or camp on another's known land, it was fine. It was only when someone showed disrespect by doing it without permission," Fire Eyes said.

My grandfather said: "Warriors have to be fierce to enemies to ensure security."

I remember how he looked at me as he said it, his head tilted toward me, his eyes spearing deeply into mine.

"A warrior must be like the-One-Who-Likes-to-Sleep-So-Much. The-One-Who-Likes-to-Sleep-So-Much is ferocious in fighting to ensure his hunting grounds are protected from trespassers," my grandfather explained to me about bears.

"They challenge other bears first. If the trespassing bear still persists in trespassing, all manner of battle is accepted so that not only he is defeated, but other bears who might have a similar idea are defeated, as well."

"But does the-One-Who-Likes-to-Sleep-So-Much torture his enemies?" I asked my grandfather.

"Good questions," suggested Great Heart.

"No. But The-One-Who-Likes-to-Sleep-So-Much isn't human and is therefore not changeable in nature. Humans are untamed in their spirits. Anything can happen when their minds are twisted. An enemy's mind that is twisted is more dangerous than any of our animal brothers."

The Mohawk mind was twisted against us. As mentioned, it hadn't been the first time that the Mohawk attacked us at Penagok. They had also attacked the village at Beskeodanak. We had always sent them away with their tails between their legs. You see we had been going back and forth at each other since before my birth but it had never really been anything more than short skirmishes. Still, the fort on the bluff at Penagok had been built to guard against the natures of one's such as them. We knew an enemy could show up in our woods at anytime. At Penagok whenever we caught wind that the Magua were in the area we would shelter at the palisade.

The great battle between the Penagok and Mohawk happened just after the Great Dying Time. I suppose they smelled death and grew hungry for more. We were weary from mourning and were caught off guard. If we had not been through the torment of watching our families and friends die from unknown reasons, we would have been prepared for them. They would never have been able to attack us.

The night before the Mohawk came the sky was stained red ochre. The sky the day the Magua appeared was deep with clouds. The Mohawk came on our lands, as they usually did, in small bands of about twenty men. It was later reported to us that they did not join together into a larger force until they were already encamped on the plain below the fort. Even then we didn't see them because they disguised themselves by hiding behind trees and using camouflage.

I later heard that on the way to Penagok that the Mohawk killed all those who they came in contact with so that their arrival would be in secret. They came in such secrecy that they were undetected even when they were camped below the palisade. Even then, we did not know how many of them had come on our lands. The attack came as a total surprise.

On the morning we saw the Magua Day Traveler was smudged against the sky like bear grease behind the clouds. The time of harvest had come and the corn had already been stored inside the palisade. People had left villages and encampments on the opposite side of the river and those who lived up river near the island where I stayed each planting season had also come to the fort to celebrate the harvest with the Green Corn Dance, feasting and visiting families and friends before setting out to their hunting wigwam.

Everything, except for the sky the day of the Mohawk attack, seemed normal and quiet. You wouldn't have been able to feel that anything was out of sorts. As I mentioned, the Mohawk had made unsuccessful raids upon the Penagok. This time, too, when we awoke and saw the Magua camped at our village below the fort it looked as though we would be able to repulse the Mohawk easily by just waiting them out as we remained secure inside the safety of our fort. But, safety is relative - if you are inside of a safe place you can expect to be safe. Leave it and your safety is gone.

The ancient palisade, which had always been a Penagok place of refuge when we were attacked, was home to over seventy wigwam, council lodge and storage. The whole was surrounded by 10 foot poles that were stuck next to each other 3 feet into the ground. Around the outside we had also dug a trench as additional protection. The palisade was built so that it overlooked the steep sand and clay bluffs and gave a view of the plains, river and valley below. It was the perfect vantage point. The perfect place to wait out an enemy.

We eyed each other for several days. I guess they figured we would be harder to fight than they had thought. They shouted insults at us, trying to engage us in battle. We did not give in to them. We also hurled insults at them.

"Go back to your women!" shouted one, referring to the fact that the Mohawks were led by women chiefs.

"False face, go back to your women so we don't bite you," shouted another.

Mohawk Assault on the Penagok

I doubt they understood us since we shouted at them in our language, Abenaki. But our meanings may well have been clear enough. In their turn the Mohawks told us, in a growling ear burning accented Abenaki: "We've come to eat. Come out so we can drink your blood and gnaw your bones!"

Some of our warriors who had been out when the Mohawk came filtered back slowly. From one of them we heard that the Mohawk had been scouting our lands over the course of several days. Although they tried to kill anyone they came into contact with the Mohawk had been routed by several villages that they came into contact with along the way to Penagok. I suppose it infuriated the Maneaters so that when they came to Penagok they were resolved to not let a single one of us survive.

After several days of daring each other, questioning each other's ancestry and abilities, neither side budged. It was when we began to believe that they'd either wait us out through the winter or would give up and go home that we suddenly spotted a single swaggering Mohawk appearing on the plains below. He walked as though he belonged on our lands, strutting like a proud tom turkey. As he strode across the plain below the fort, he did so slowly, deliberately, tweeking our honor. It brought fire to the anger of young Penacook warriors.

"Maneater, go back to your land or I'll crush your skull like a pumpkin!," cried out one.

"Coward! Come closer so I can see your eyes as you die!," shouted another.

I, too, was angry. Looking out through the poles you would have thought that the Mohawk were still encamped directly across the river from the palisade. But you, like we Penagok, would have been misled.

Perturbed by this single Mohawk's behavior and thinking he was alone, several of my friends pushed the branches and twigs that had barricaded the entranceway and rushed out the palisade to capture the wayward Maqua. But, as the entranceway was cleared of the barriers and the men left the palisade's safety, the whole Mohawk force rushed into the palisade from out of nowhere. We were totally unprepared for their overwhelming force. They must have snuck around the backside where the banking wasn't so steep. As we realized our mistake we also realized it would take all our energy to fight for our survival and then push them back to their lands. The Mohawk had crossed the river in stealth and quickly broke through our defenses. It was like water swelling over and absorbing sand. The Mohawk screamed their taunts and insults at us, their painted faces contorted to frighten our spirits, the ball headed clubs swinging like extensions of their arms as the raged toward us. Penagok men and women rushed into wigwams to retrieve weapons, only to be struck down by arrows as their backs bent into wigwam entrances, or their heads smashed as they came out.

The battle raged on and on with neither side willing to give up. For us it was life or death. For the Magua it started with their wanting our deaths but became clear to them that we would not allow them to win. Realizing this they fought with vengeance against us for their own lives. I led my people, urging them on when it seemed we'd lose. I shouted: "We owe it to the seven generations before and after us. The Magua can't be allowed to stay here! Suck the blood from the blood suckers!!"

We were fighting for our existence. For our families. For our winter store of food. Arrows found their mark, thrusting their stony and boney sharp edges into muscles, sinew and veins. Skulls

Mohawk Assault on the Penagok

cracked like frozen squash from tomahawks and head crushers. Everywhere blood drenched grandmother land making her fat as the men's dying life energy swelled her. Warriors knees buckled and men fell to their deaths off the sand and clay bluffs, screams and war cries mixing with each other until neither was heard distinctly above the din. Bright red ochre mixed with the bears blood that had earlier stained the birches, maples and oaks, while the pine of peace stood green above us. The smell of blood, smoke and rage filled the land. The Morôdemak was red.

It became clear that neither side would win. We fought with all our strength as Day Traveler tread the trail above us. We battled on and on until the Mohawk, weakened by our relentless defense and we by our determination not to lose, started to retreat back to the river. As they ran, sprinted, fumbled and tumbled over the edge of the bluff, we let them go. They headed into their waiting canoes that had been covered from our eyes by branches in the marshy land below the fort. Exhausted eyes followed their specks as they headed upriver, paddling with all their might. We didn't chase them. So many had been lost. We headed for the pine barren behind the palisade to seek safety.

In the end, the battle had been a stalemate. A draw until the next time. We wouldn't forget what they did to us, and likewise, they wouldn't forget that we hadn't let them win. Behind the palisade at the burial grounds and on the plain below the steep banking bodies of Penagok and Magua were left where they lie together. There was no time for more than a hasty burial. We were unsure of when they might return. There was no telling whether reinforcements had arrived from across the Gwenitegw.

From that time on we were wary that the Magua would return; but we, too, put them on alert. They knew that we would seek retribution for their attack on us. You would also want revenge for an enemy who attacked you when you were at your weakest. You would have no respect for such an enemy and would wait for your chance. That was how we felt. In the end more than 350 Penagok and 350 Magua were killed

"350 Mohawk," noted Great Heart in amazement.

"How did they make such a long journey with so many men? What did they eat?" asked Scorching Tail.

"You are right. A warrior's first battle is hunger," said Gray Ears.

Fire Eyes explained: "They attacked all who they met along the way, eating whatever they found in the defeated village. Each Mohawk warrior also brought ground-parched corn flour that they ate as is, or mixed with clean water. They also hunted along the way.

"So many men. They weren't noticed as they traveled from the Hudson to the Morôdemak?" asked Matted Fur.

"No," Fire Eyes said. "They were masters of stealth. They moved silent as deer but fought as ferociously as a hungry bear."

Matted Fur looked over at Scorching Tail clawing a berry: "Yes. We know all about hungry bears!"

Among those killed were Penagok women, children, old people and warriors. We lost so many brave people. I lost many of my family that day. Aunts, uncles, cousins. Friends. The bluff became a sacred site. Sacred land. Nwaskw. Nwaskw where so much blood was absorbed by grandmother land. It was to become our new stronghold. Our heart in the winters to come.

Fire Eyes concluded: "The palisade is long gone. The land sanctified by the drenching of human lives into the soil is still there, ab-

Mohawk Assault on the Penagok

sorbed long ago when clay, sand, water and blood intermingled. But, its importance has been forgotten by the people who travel Route 393 up Sugar Ball Bluff at Concord, New Hampshire.

Land of the Shapeshifter

5

The "First" to the Top of Agiocochook

(1642 C.E.)

In 1642 Governor John Winthrop of Massachusetts Bay Colony recorded in his Journal that Darby Field, "an Irishman, living about Piscat, being accompanied with two Indians, went to the top of White Hill."   From that simple statement, followed a few lines later with "...and his two Indians took courage by his example and went with him" it is clear that Darby Field wasn't, as many claim, the first person to climb Mt. Washington. Field was accompanied by two Native Americans. What is significant about it being two Native Americans is that these two men climbed what was considered to their people to be sacred ground, a place, according to Winthrop's Journal, that "no Indian ever dared to go higher, and he would die if he went." Who's to say that other Native Americans hadn't climbed it even earlier than the recorded event? The following is my interpretative account of that "first" climb to the top of Agiocochook "Place of the Great Storm Spirit" - known today as Mt. Washington.

"You are going to do what?" asked Woman-of-the-Pines to her son, Standing Moose, as she continued stirring a rabbit stew in the pot suspended from a tripod above the fire.

"Climb Agiocochook," answered Standing Moose.

"Climb Agiocochook?! She responded, dumbfounded as she stopped mid stir, disbelieving that her ears had heard her son correctly. Standing Moose who had already seen sixteen winters must be loosing his mind, she thought, or playing a joke.

"Why?" His mother inquired, "Would anyone want to go up" pointing with her chin and eyes toward the cloud shrouded bulk lurking against the western horizon, "there unless they were Medôlinôwinno (a person of medicine) - or out of their mind? They'll die." She then said in half whispers, lest the bad spirit living up there could hear her:

"You don't have the power to withstand Maji Nwaskw who lives up there."

"I'm going with several others."

"Who?"

"A white man from Piscataqua, White Skunk, and..."

"White Skunk?! I might have known! And why would you go there with a white man? Does he have some special power to protect you?"

"No."

She had to admit though; he was the first white man she'd met. He'd caused quite a stir when he walked into the village of two hundred Pigwacket people. She'd heard about the trouble the white people were causing in the land south of the Penagok, and even to the Penagok, but she'd never seen one – or for that matter smelled one. From what she could smell, they seem to not know to use water and sand to scrub themselves of sweat or smear their skin with bears grease. A long time ago she'd also heard from her father that they possessed powers. Powers like fire and thunder which they controlled in their hands. But now others had that

The "First" to the Top of Agiocochook

power which they had traded furs to get. Now even some Pigwackets had guns.

"But why go up?"

"The white man is looking for shining rocks," he responded. Beyond that he didn't know.

"Shining rocks? There are plenty everywhere, look!," she said, pointing to mica encrusted quartz boulders nearby. Woman-of-the-Pines continued to look at her son.

"So he's on a rock hunt? And you, why do you go?"

Indeed it did sound stupid to him. But, he didn't know Darby was looking for diamonds or silver. Those things were valuable in Europe and worth climbing a mountain for, even if you warn them about bad spirits living on top.

"I still don't understand why 'you' are going and you just stand and gawk at me like a deer watching an arrow come at it. Perhaps you are all bewitched or just plain crazy" she said, setting the wooden handled giant clam shell atop a rock next to the fire.

The Pigwacket village was located near the "Zaw-kw-tegok" known now as the "Saco" River and was not far, as a hawk flies, from the foot of Agiocochook. But on most late spring and summer days Agiocochook could barely be seen at the village. And it was late spring, just past raspberry picking time. The mountain usually covered itself with too much haze and clouds. It was during the winter moons that it showed itself as it really was, standing out as a boney hulk against the icy sky.

Mountains, as well as rivers, balanced boulders, great lakes, some people with special powers, and the ancestors were Nwaskwomak.

Nwaskwomak were spirits. Nwaskwomak could be good or they could be bad. The spirit atop Agiocochook was known to be bad. The evidence was the angry storms that showed its power. Other mountains had power, too. Atop them lived the thunder birds, the badôgiak. But the badôgiak were, by and large, easier to get along with than the Maji Nwaskw. Badôgiak could be satiated with respect and offerings. The Maji Nwaskw couldn't.

"Why indeed go up?" he thought now that he was shivering and wet through to the bear skin slimed against his back due to sweat, causing what smelled like bear musk to float to his nose with each blast of wind that was hurled at him by Maji Nwaskw. His joints ached each and every time he thrust a leg up another rock. Ascending the mountain hadn't been easy. He was used to walking trails that twisted, turned, were muddy in late autumn and early spring, and up and around boulder strewn paths to get to the best hunting sites along mountain ridges, but this was beyond anything he'd experienced before. It was like he'd entered a new land. Yet he saw in front of him that the climb was nearly over. Something was there. Something inexpressible.

A while ago they had left the last of the spruce and had passed over what looked like open land covered here and there with moss and plants the likes of which he'd never seen before. They'd also passed two deep valleys in which snow glimmered at them from far below. In looking through the intermittent clouds at the land below them they had noticed something that looked for all they could tell like a giant snake. Darby had said it was a river. It could be a great snake - Gchi skog. Who knew? At that point a howling wind pushed down at them and the group that had set out from Pigwacket would go no further, leaving just Standing Moose, White Skunk and Field to continue the journey.

"You will be killed," one of those who remained behind said to White Skunk and Standing Moose. "This man is possessed by

The "First" to the Top of Agiocochook

Maji Nwaskw." Maji Nwaskw — the Bad Spirit. "Don't go with him" they urged. "Leave him to his fate!"

But Standing Moose dreamed last night and the dream wasn't a warning. Dreams would tell you what to do. The dream had been a good dream. White Skunk said that his dream had been good, too.

When he thought about it Standing Moose realized that the dreams for the last several moons had been the same. In it he'd seen a beautiful woman. He'd also seen children. He thought of Mist-on-the-Hill and knew it had to be her that he'd dreamed about. It warmed him to think of her. No, he knew you could trust what the dreams told you. He knew that after he returned he'd ask her to set up a wigwam together with him. Dreams like that don't prophesize that something bad will happen to you.

In determination upward they went. Most of the way after they left their companions was spent walking in and out of clouds and mist. Darby kept looking at the ground for his shining rocks, inspecting some every once in a while, placing some in a bag he carried. Below them, through a hole in the mists, they had also glimpsed a great lake that he and White Skunk thought must be Wiwninibesaki - the Land around the Lakes. From time to time, Field had to rest so they did too, sitting on perpetually wet rocks, trying the best they could to keep warm. As they walked he could smell his mother's stew and wished it was in him instead of the handful of parched corn.

"Maji Nwaskw is not happy with us," White Skunk commented, his eyes constantly darting back and forth to scan the sky, wondering when the bad spirit would swoop down and gather them up.

"Are you scared?," Standing Moose teased. "I thought you were brave?!" he teased, knowing that questioning White Skunk's courage was what his friend needed to embolden him.

But as he listened to White Skunk, Standing Moose still didn't know why he did it. Perhaps the adventure of it. Perhaps because White Skunk was his best friend and he always did what he thought White Skunk wanted to do. White Skunk was always the troublemaker. Anyway, he'd always been curious to see Agiocochook up close, but he knew the danger. Not that danger stopped any real man. Didn't he scout around a Mohawk camp intent on raiding? And they were known as "Magua," or "Maneaters" in Abenaki. Then again, now that he thought about it, White Skunk had encouraged him to do that, as well. The trouble maker! Still, Agiocochook was much more serious than the threat of being eaten alive by a Mohawk. It was the home of Maji Nwaskw - the Bad Spirit. It was never climbed. Well, it had been - not to see what was on top or for the purpose of looking for shining rocks that you could find anywhere, though. It had been climbed, according to his grandfather, by persons of medicine who did it shortly after a fiery arrow shot across the sky and the sky had turned dark during mid day.

"Great Chief Babiwseso-Ogawinno had seen it in a dream and it happened," his grandfather said.

He had heard other stories of shamans who headed out for the summit, but they'd never returned. One man did return, now he thought of it, but he'd gone mad. But generally speaking no Pigwacket, Wiwninibesaki, Penagok, or any other people climbed above the tree lines. Not even a Mohawk would do it. To do so would anger the thunder beings who lived atop the peaks. Still he and his friend had set out to climb it. Maybe, he guessed, they wanted to prove their manhood. The man they climbed with, Darby Field, had seen 32 winters. He spoke the language of the

The "First" to the Top of Agiocochook

Massachusetts which was mostly understandable. But he never was really able to explain his reasons enough for them to understand. No, they never did figure out why he wanted to climb. Darby had said something about shiny stones and silver. But he couldn't translate exactly what it was he was hoping to find - something like "tee-ah-men" or something like that. Neither White Skunk nor Standing Moose could understand. Darby had carried something that looked like white birch bark and used a small stick to draw on it symbols of which they had no idea the meaning. He was a strange sort of fellow, as were all white men who did things without much meaning. More and more of them, he heard from the Penagok when he went to the Place of the Falling Bank, had come to the flat land in the south. There were also the Français to the north. They were becoming more and more like ants crawling across the land looking for food. Field, he knew, lived at a white settlement near Zobagw - the ocean. He didn't know much else.

Eventually they passed two ponds among the rocks, one of black water, the other red like blood. The sight gave them chills.

"Maybe this is the lake created when Gluskab shot an arrow into the sky," White Skunk said to Standing Moose. Standing Moose agreed it must be. Long ago, in contest with Mekomwiso, Gluskab, the Abenaki cultural hero who had also made the Ash Tree People, the Abenaki, had shot his arrow at Agiocochook and it made a hole in grandfather sky. At night you could see this hole as the evening star. This hole was the lake.

The higher the small group climbed, the more their chests pounded like drums in their ears and their hearts raced as if in anticipation of something awesome. The mists grew darker and denser, but they continued onward, ever upward.

"We've entered the land of dreams?" commented White Skunk. "This gray is like in dreams. Maybe we are in a nightmare?"

Land of the Shapeshifter

Standing Moose couldn't help but agree. It was unnerving.

They clamored upward, stubbing their moccasin covered toes against quartz boulders, jamming them in between cracks and crevices, and sliding on slimy gravel. Sometimes they nearly tripped and fell, but they quickly righted themselves, so worried were they that they'd fall off the mountainside, or, that the bad spirit would snatch them away if they showed fear. They wouldn't give into fear. Standing Moose was firm in that. Even when he underwent his vision high atop a hill, he didn't let into fear. During the four days and nights without food and spent in reflection and prayer inside a stone circle, he didn't give in to fear. He'd received his vision and was accepted by his spirit protector throughout the rest of his life. Moose had come to him. He knew then that even if the Maji Nwaskw tried to terrorize him, he could live up to that challenge. Moose was a powerful spirit protector.

Without warning the gray cleared and Day Traveler appeared above them. Soon they reached the top not realizing they had done it. The clouds that had concealed their goal all day gradually lifted and in front of them they saw a flat gravel area with nothing higher in front except of course boulders strewn about everywhere. They walked forward a bit further then stood and looked all around them. The land spread out beneath them. The Bad Spirit was no where to be seen.

"Maybe he took off?" suggested Standing Moose.

"Perhaps."

"Maybe the smell of the white man was too strong for his nose," added Standing Moose.

White Skunk smiled his response.

The "First" to the Top of Agiocochook

Both White Skunk and Standing Moose remained on full alert, their eyes as round as the protective stone amulets they wore on leather straps around their necks. In a valley below them they noticed the sun no longer shone, and darkness had crept in.

"Perhaps Maji Nwaskw is down there in the valley where Day Traveler no longer walks," White Skunk suggested.

Standing Moose agreed. If Maji Nwaskw wasn't atop the mountain, he probably was in a valley, perhaps the one that was now covered in darkness. Whatever the case, Standing Moose and White Skunk were unable to relax until Field headed back down the mountain.

Before heading down the mountain Field picked up a few quartz crystals and put them in his pack. Standing Moose and White Skunk looked at each other.

"You should not just take the stones. You must make an offering of tobacco to the stones" said Standing Moose.

Field ignored them.

"Maji Nwaskw will punish him," Standing Moose said to White Skunk. "He will go crazy."

White Skunk and Standing Moose each placed a bit of tobacco atop the stone covered ground and asked forgiveness from the stone people. Although they worried the offering might be rejected, they also placed a tobacco offering to Maji Nwaskw, begging his forgiveness for their trespass. If he accepted the offering they would be alive tomorrow. If he accepted it they would not go insane. Field laughed at them and told them it was the white man's God who protected them not a tobacco offering.

Land of the Shapeshifter

It was never prudent to laugh at spirits, even if they weren't at home.

The journey back to their village was uneventful. Before leaving Darby asked them to accompany him back up Agiocochook during the next moon. Since nothing bad had happened to them the first time, they agreed. During the next moon Standing Moose and White Skunk returned again to climb Agiocochook. Three other men came with them to pick quartz crystals. Again Field and the three other white men made no offering to the stones.

"He will go crazy," White Skunk predicted as he and Standing Moose offered tobacco to the stones and Maji Nwaskw.

Seven winters would pass but, as White Skunk predicted, Darby Field, like the shaman who had returned from the top of Agiocochook, went insane and died.

"Maji Nwaskw has had his revenge," Standing Moose said to White Skunk.

They each faced Agiocochook and made an offering of tobacco. Neither of them ever climbed Agiocochook again.

6

Crows

(1659 C.E.)

It's the year 1659. Captain Richard Walderne (Waldron), in response to an invitation from the Penagok Confederation Chief Passaconaway, is traveling to Penagok, the capitol of the Penagok Confederation. Walderne believes the invitation was extended to him because he is one of the major trading partners of the Penagok. The real reason is that Passaconaway has learned Walderne is instrumental in urging Puritan settlement of Penagok.

It has been almost 24 years since the 39 year old Walderne began trading with the Penagok. By 1663 Walderne and Peter Coffin will set up a fur trading post at Penagok, not more than a few yards from a Penagok fort as well as the site of Passaconaway's summer lodge at Sewell's Island.

The 109 year old Passaconaway has recently been informed by his contacts outside Boston that the English plan to settle at the Confederation capitol. In fact, a request for settlement has already been submitted to Boston. Among those whose names appear on the petition is Richard Walderne who has long claimed to be the best friend of the Penagok. Other Dover and Newbury residents desiring to settle at Penagok are none other than Peter Coffin and another whose family shall feature prominently in the annals of Penagok and settler relations, Jonathon Heard. The Deputy Governor of Massachusetts Bay Colony, Thomas Danforth who in 1692 becomes involved with the Salem Witch trials and who, incidentally is also the brother to Jonathon Danforth, the chief surveyor for Massachusetts Bay Colony, judges the settlement request meet. The petition states:

> "To the Honored Generall Courte, now assembled at Boston.
>
> "The humble petecyon of us whose names are underwritten, beinge inhabytants of this jurisdiction, and beinge senseable of the need of multeplyinge of towneshippes for the inlargement of the contrey, and accommodateinge of such as want opportunity to improve themselves, have taken into consideration a place which is called Pennecooke, which by reporte is a place fit for such an one - Now the humble request of your petetioners to this honred Courte is, that we may have the grant of a trackte of land their to the quantity of twelve miles square, which being granted, we shall give up ourselves to be at the cost and charge of vewinge of it, and consider fully aboute it, wheather to proceed on for the settlinge of a towne or noe, and for that end shall crave the liberty of three yeares to give in our resolution; and in case that wee due proseed, then our humble request is, that we may have the grant of our freedome from publique charge for the space of seaven yeares after the time of our resolution given in to this Honred Court, for our encorragement to settle a plantation soe furre remote as knowinge that many will be our inconveniences (for a longe time) which we must expeckt to meet with all, which desires of ours beinge answered, your petetioners shall ever pray for the happiness of this Honred Courte, and rest your humble petetioners."

The May 18, 1659 response by the committee regarding the request was entered:

"The Committee do judge meet that the petitioners be granted a plantation of eight miles square, upon condition that at the sessions of the Generall Court to be held in Octo. 1660, they make report to that Court of their resolution to p'secute the same with a competent no. of meet persons that will ingage to carry on the work of the said place in all civill and eclesiasticall respects, and that within two years then next ensuing there be 20 families there settled. Also that they may have imunity from all publique charges (excepting in cases extraordinary) for seven yeares next ensuing the date hereof."

The fact that Penagok is already settled by Penagok peoples and that it is the confederation capitol is of no consequence to the Boston officials. None of this information is lost on Passaconaway who is also not surprised. In addition to Passaconaway's anger at Walderne's duplicitous behavior for masquerading as a true friend of the Penagok while at the same time submitting a petition to settle at Penagok itself, the Confederation Chief fears the attempted settlement at the heart and soul of the Penagok homeland by the English will break the current peace between the Penagok and English peoples: a peace that he has struggled hard to maintain. Passaconaway decides to meet Walderne and to, as he has done so effectively with the English authorities for years now, keep him off balance by finding a way that will make Walderne desire trade more than settlement.

"Will Walderne prefer trade more than land?" asks Gray Bear during council with Passaconaway prior to the arrival of Walderne.

"Who knows the English mind? But I believe it will waylay him for a while, long enough for us to consider other options" responds Passaconaway.

"Walderne is greedy and wants power to control other people. He would trade his own mother if he could profit from it" adds Standing Moose.

"And therein lies my concern" says Gray Bear.

"And mine" Passaconaway concurs as he gazes ahead of him, past the smoldering coals in front of him, past the children playing outside, past the palisade trunks to where the land drops to the river one hundred feet below. Except for the sudden sharp shouts of chastising crows, all is silent.

"Walderne is arriving" says Passaconaway.

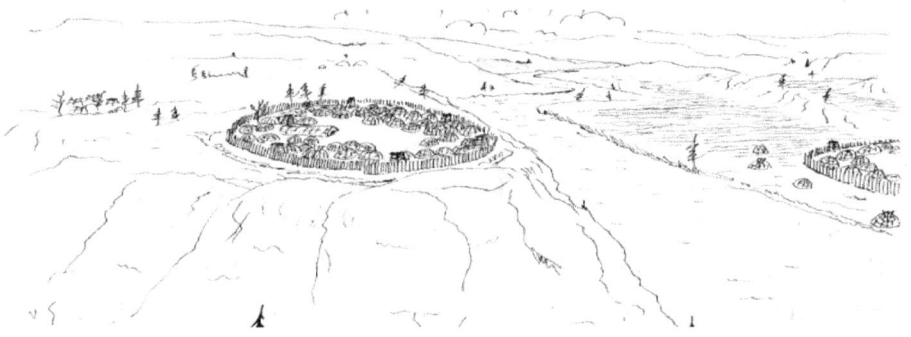

Penakok palisade at Sugar Ball Bluff and Fort Eddy Plain circa 1659 C.E.

It's mid-summer. The Strawberry Festival has already come and gone and the season of blueberries has begun. Bending through fields of ripening corn, squash and beans, the Morôdemak is calm with not even a dimple creasing the mica like surface of the wide river. Although the land and water were tranquil, the same could not be said for the cacophony that had come from the sky. The sky had been alive with the excited voices of eastern phoebes, chickadees and low flying robins. Suddenly the air was stilled by the

CROWS

screech of a red tail hawk circling beyond the eye's reach. Eastern phoebes, chickadees and robins scattered for the cover of low branch hemlocks, leaving only the crows behind. Crows are smart birds. Crows aren't easily duped by blue jays impersonating hawks. Clever little birds the blue jays that enjoy harassing smaller birds so as to steal their seeds, but they are as nothing compared to the sacred crow.

At a wigwam just outside the palisade, an old woman sits on her haunches, flattening a porcupine quill with her teeth so that it can fit into the designated holes she has made on a birch bark container. Her grand daughter kneels nearby, using a stone scraper to clean a deerskin stretched on a wooden frame.

"Listen! Do you hear the angry voice of the crow person?"

Her grand daughter cocks her ear to the sky.

"Yes."

"He's warning all the crows in the area to be alert for a bad human. It must be the white men coming to see Gchi Zôgemô (the Great Chief)," says the old woman.

"Ahô," replies her grand daughter.

Although Captain Walderne and his entourage, among whom are 14 year old Thomas Paine and 28 year old Peter Coffin, are still a distance away from the old woman and her grand daughter, the sound of the crow shouting to its fellows, has alerted the Penagok to the white men's arrival.

The old lady continues:

LAND OF THE SHAPESHIFTER

"Always show respect to the crow people. The crow people have a long memory and recall every human face they see. He-who-likes-to-sleep-so-well (bears) recall people and scents, but the crow people's ability is very keen. When the crow person recognizes someone who has treated them wrong, they call out "Caw-aw-ah" as loud as they can so that all crow people in the area know that human who wronged a crow person is near. The word is carried far and wide so that eventually even though the crow person who had met the malefactor is nowhere around, others who have recognized the human's face will carry on the warning every time the human is seen."

The old woman continues:

"I've heard the English kill the crow people because they consider them pests. Crows remember. I've heard that wherever an English settler travels, crows announce their arrival to other crows beforehand. Therefore, the Penagok know that a non-Indian has come onto their land. The call of a crow therefore gives away the presence of the English."

"Ahô."

Noses twitch at the arrival of the dark wool wearing Puritans followed by their sharp clipped voices.

"Yes, I can smell them now," says the old woman as she looks over and scrutinizes the white men.

"I've heard these white men like to wallow in their own sweat and stink" the grandmother added. "My nose now knows that what is said about them is true. They stink like a skunk!"

In the distance Walderne, Paine and Coffin appear with a Penagok guide who walks well ahead of them. The travel from Dover to

Penagok was hard going. During the summer, the sun is unrelenting, the days hot and humid. The Penagok guide had done his best to stay downwind from his charges.

"Nine months of winter; a month of rain, a month of mud, and a month where you wander across the face of the sun," Coffin notes sourly.

"What use is land like this," Paine asks, scuffing through the sandy soil. "Only runty pines grow here."

"That's because you've yet to see the river beyond the palisade. The land below the bluff is fat" says Walderne.

"Will the authorities at Boston allow settlement at Penagok? Doesn't New Hampshire claim jurisdiction here?" asked Paine.

"Both claim jurisdiction but remember Boston sent two expeditions up the Morôdemak to find its source and lay out its boundaries. New Hampshire has not done the same. Boston's claim to the land is therefore legal. That's why I suggested we submit our petition to Boston. Besides New Hampshire won't protect settlers at Penagok, but Boston, wanting to maintain a presence this far upriver, will" said Walderne.

At this point a crow swoops down close to the party, landing nearby to begin squawking at the men.

"Bloody crows! First thing I'd do is exterminate the lot of them!" says Paine as he kicks a stone at one. The crow relents and darts toward the top of a nearby pine. From its perch it screeches at other crows until a crow concert ensues.

Walderne and his men reach the palisade from the south east. They are careful to avoid the above-ground cemetery located just east of the palisade.

"A good location for a palisade" Coffin comments, his eyes scanning the horizon where the Penagok's totem mountain, Gôwizawajo, rises.

Walderne explains:

"This place is known by two names: 'Place of the Falling Bank' because the sandy soil gives way beneath your feet, and also 'At the Bend in the River' because of the crookedness of the river here that nearly bends back on itself. The soil is very fat and good for crops," remarked Walderne, as he took off his hat and wiped his brow. It was his intention to settle on this land himself if Boston would really allow it.

The group heads to the palisade entrance where a Penagok delegation waits to bring them to the council lodge. Inside the lodge, a number of elderly and middle aged men sit around the periphery of the walls on mats covering the ground. Toward the back of the lodge, seated on a bear fur behind the fire pit in the place of honor is the Great Chief, Passaconaway. The men are all chiefs. The chief of the Wiwninibesaki, the Bemijijoasek, the Pigwacket, the Nashua and others. They have all come to hear their chief speak with Walderne.

Passaconaway is no fool. He's been one of the major powerbrokers in the northeast since before the Pilgrims landed at Patuxet. He knows that Walderne is a powerful man, one who has influence with the authorities at Boston. To beat such a man at his own game, Passaconaway must be like the crow who, after the blue jay scares all other birds away with his imitation of a bird of prey, then scares away the blue jay. The Great Chief also knows that if he wants to prevent Penagok from being taken by Boston, he must make Walderne desire something more than land. For that reason, he invited the chiefs who make up the confederation he founded over forty winters ago.

The make up of the assemblage is not lost on Walderne as he recognizes some of the chiefs from near Oyster River. As he and his companion take their place on the mats, they are offered pine needle tea and corn meal fried in bear fat which is then sweetened with maple syrup.

"The Great Chief welcomes you," begins the translator. "He trusts that your journey was a good one."

"Very good, gchi wliwni," responds Walderne, thanking the Great Chief in Abenaki, the language of the Penagok.

Passaconaway is the quintessential diplomat. He never comes directly to the point, especially in dealings with the English. After polite conversation about each others welfare and those of family, the crops and the weather, Passaconaway broaches his real reason for asking Walderne to Penagok.

"You've been a trusted friend to the Penagok peoples for almost twenty winters. During this time our peoples have mutually benefited from the friendship," begins the Great Chief who continues. Walderne listens intently.

"In light of this friendship I've discussed with the council and we've agreed to make you an offer. The Penagok Confederation invites you to build a trading station here at the Confederation capitol."

Passaconaway stops to measure Walderne's response. Walderne's face shows he is pleased.

Land of the Shapeshifter

"We are aware that Englishmen would like to trade directly with us, as well," says Passaconaway who then stops again to measure Walderne's response.

Walderne's eyebrows rise. It was clear at that moment to Passaconaway that Walderne hadn't thought of that.

"Clever blue jay outwitted himself," Passaconaway thought to himself regarding Walderne.

The Great Chief continues:

"This is why we invite you first, our good friend. We fear, though we know you'd never let it happen since you are our good friend and you would lose the exclusive right to trade with us if a settlement happened here, that if Boston were to ever send settlers to Penagok that such a settlement would change our trading arrangements. You would no longer have profit since there would be too much competition. A fur trading post here at Penagok would also be advantageous for the Wiwninibesaki, Bemijijoasek, Pigwacket and others who now must travel far to Dover to trade."

Passaconaway sizes up Walderne's response. It is clear from his eager face and shifting eyes that Walderne is very interested in the Penagok proposal. But Walderne is no fool.

"My petition has been found out by the Penagok," he realizes. Thinking fast Walderne determines to himself:

"I'll accept the Penagok proposal and for now will not push the settlement petition to be reviewed by the General Court next year. The Boston authorities weren't really excited about the prospect of considering settlement at Penagok anyway with Mason grant friends in London potentially stirring things up with the king. No, I will wait and try again later at a more fortuitous time. "

Walderne glances toward Coffin who nods agreement with his business partner, Walderne.

Never mind the other petitioners who had desired settlement. Walderne's needs are first in his mind. They can fend for themselves.

"I accept your generous offer," says Walderne.

Passaconaway smiles.

"He'll just bide his time, while we will be as the crow to the blue jay," thinks Passaconaway. He offers Walderne the pipe.

Passaconaway knows Walderne will not give up his desire for settlement. But as with the crow screeching to his fellow crows, so has Passaconaway warned his people of what is coming. So too will the Penagok be on their guard against the English.

Land of the Shapeshifter

7

A Petition for Land

(1662 C.E.)

On April 9, 1662, the Great Chief of the Penagok, Passaconaway (Babiwseso-Ogawinno), petitioned the General Court of Massachusetts for a piece of land. His request was granted and he was given land north of the Souhegan River. The land, which would be north of Horseshoe Pond in present day Litchfield, was one and a half miles wide and three miles long and extended along both sides of the Morôdemak River. Included in the grant were two river islands known for a time as Nunnehaha and Minnewawa and later as Reed's Island which are located in the northern section of Merrimack, New Hampshire.

The topmost branches of the white pines lining the Morôdemak River moved in unison to the northeasterly breeze blowing off the water. The destination of Massachusetts Bay Colony's chief surveyor, Jonathon Danforth, lay dead ahead of him. The chief surveyor had been sent by the Massachusetts General Court in response to Penagok Chief Passaconaway's petition for land. The land he requested, in an odd twist of fate, had belonged to his people since the end of the last Ice Age. When I say belonged I mean that they had been custodians of the land. No Penagok would ever presume to claim they "owned" land. The petition stated:

> "To the honerd John Endecot Esqr together with the rest of the honerd General Court now Assembled in Boston the petition of papisseconnewa in behalf of himself as also of many other Indians who now for a longe time o'r selves o'r

progenators seated upon a tract of land called Naticot and is now in the possession of Mr. William Brenton of Rode Island marchant; and is confirmed to the said Mr. Brenton to him his heir and assigns according to the Laws of this Jurisdiction, by reason of which tracte of land being taken up as a foresaid, and thereby yr pore petitionir with many oth (ers is) in an onsetled condition and must be forced in a short time to remove to some other place.

"The Humble request of yr petitionr is that this honerd Courte wolde pleas to grante vnto vs a parcell of land for or comfortable cituation; to be stated for or Injoyment; as also for the comfort of oths after vs; as also that this honerd Court wold pleas to take in to yr serious and grave consideration the condition and also the requeste of yr pore Supliant and to a poynte two or three persons as a Committee to Ar (range wi) th sum one or two Indians to vew and determine of some place and to Lay out the same, not further to trouble this honerd Assembly, humbly cravinge an expected answer this present sesion I shall re main yr humble Servante

"Wherein yu Shall commande
"PAPISSECONEWA.
"Boston: 8:3 mo 1662."

The petition was, in effect, the Great Chief's hope that the English would be generous enough to allow him to die on a piece of his own land. He made the request not knowing whether or not his wish would be fulfilled.

Along the Morôdemak, not far from a pair of river islands, Standing Birch and Running Moose sat atop a rock, looking out at the sunlight dancing across the wavelets.

"It's ironic" Standing Birch said.

A Petition for Land

Running Moose, who was taking some parched cornmeal out of a deerskin pouch attached to his waist, looked over at Standing Birch.

"How do you mean?" Running Moose asked, placing a bit of the cornmeal in his mouth.

"Our Gchi Zôgemô (Great Chief) reduced to begging the English for land that by all rights is his. His clan had used that land for generations."

"Oh, that. Yes. You have a good point. It is ironic," Running Bear responded then added: "But we live in a time of irony."

"True. Look at our interaction with these English during these past forty odd winters. Every agreement our chief has made with the English at Boston has been broken. The Great Chief made land use agreements with the English to share parts of the land we have lived on, hunted on, and fished since the time when the snows wouldn't stop. What did the English do? They took the land as their own and forbid anyone from using it except them! The English then built fences and refused to allow us on those lands to hunt and fish," Standing Birch said.

Running Moose nodded his head in agreement and swallowed. He squinted toward the river as if looking for something and then turned to Standing Birch.

"The English have taken away our lands piece by piece." Running Moose began.

"As soon as they take a piece of land they shove a piece of white birch bark at us that they say is a grant from their government and then order us from our ancient hunting grounds. When we question them, they say it is lawful, whatever that means to them. If we press hard they say their king gave them our land because no one lived on it. Now tell me, Standing Birch, how we Penagok can win with logic like that! Our Great Chief knew they were illogical over forty winters ago when he urged peace with these troublemakers. He knew it but he also knew we had to live with them or the Mohawk would never leave us alone. Now we know that the Mohawk would have been better to live with than the English have proved to be!"

Running Moose then stepped off the rock and stooped down toward the water. He pulled out a carved gourd that hung to his belt from a piece of rawhide. He then used the gourd to scoop some water to drink.

Standing Birch hadn't been listening. He was preoccupied with the anger that was boiling up inside of him every time he thought of English duplicity. He jumped off the rock and stood next to Running Moose:

"The English even plan to take Penagok!" Standing Birch said. "It is intolerable! Penagok is our heartland. It is N'dakinna! Our land!"

Running Moose began shaking with anger at the thought of the English stealing the Penagok peoples' heartland.

"Who told you this?!" Running Moose demanded.

"I heard it from White-as-Snow. She overheard the Great Chief telling his son." Standing Birch said.

"See what has happened since we submitted to English authority! They reward us for being their ally by stealing everything we have and leaving us as nothing more than beggars on our own land!" Running Moose responded.

A Petition for Land

At that moment Running Moose and Standing Birch looked up at the same time to see a canoe floating toward the islands in the middle of the river. Seated in the canoe were two white men who, Running Moose and Standing Birch assumed without acknowledging it to each other, were the surveyors.

Without changing topic, Standing Birch added:

"Eventually we'll have no choice but to fight them to get our land back. We'll have to push the English back into the sea and reclaim our place."

Running Moose looked toward him and said:

"Yes. In just 18 winters since the Great Chief agreed to ally with the English our tribe, the most feared along the Morôdemak has become a group of fearful old men who do their best to reign in their angry young men who are looking for a fight."

Standing Birch and Running Moose then headed for their canoe to join the Great Chief as he met the English. Passaconaway was waiting on the larger of the two islands. Standing Birch and Running Moose had tried to dissuade Passaconaway from attending, but the Great Chief was determined to personally meet the surveyors.

Passaconaway was taller than most Penagok. That said a lot. Most Penagok were tall and stately in appearance, with shimmering dark hair and eyes. The skin tone of the Penagok was the color of the brown ash tree due to the bear's grease that they smeared on their skin for protection from insects and the cold as well as by the tannin from oak leaves used to protect their skin from the sun. Passaconaway was by now well over 100 years old. Muscles still shaped his arms, legs and chest. Atop his chest a tattoo of a bear moved with each breath the great chief took. Even to the most weak minded Passaconaway was a sight to behold with his bear skin cape, bear claw necklace, and turkey feather coronet atop his long flowing, snow white hair.

In truth, Passaconaway was surprised to see the surveyors. Yes, he had been told by messenger that someone would come and that it would happen on this day, but it did surprise him that the English were actually going to follow-through on his request. One winter had, after all, already passed without word of whether his request would elicit a response from the General Court. His petition had elicited a response. Now it was to be seen if what he had asked for would be given to him.

A few minutes after Running Moose and Standing Birch reached the island several white men alighted from their canoes and moved toward Passaconaway.

"This is the Chief Surveyor, Jonathan Danforth," a tall man named Parker said to the Great Chief. "He has been sent by the General Court to survey in response to your request for land."

Parker moved to one side as Danforth moved to stand in front of Passaconaway.

Passaconaway sized up the man in front of him. Danforth had the skin color of rainbow trout flesh, hair like the sun and eyes the color of water. The Great Chief noticed that Danforth did have an honest and friendly face, something which in his experience he hadn't often found in the English he had met thus far. In particular he thought of the bob-and-weave personality traits that made Major Waldron a suspicious and disliked character. He had met with Major Waldron three winters ago. Waldron had been amiable and pliable at the time, but by now had not only set up a trading post at Penagok, which Passaconaway had agreed to, but also, according

A Petition for Land

to the great chief's sources, was again seeking, along with other white men at Salem, to obtain all the land at Penagok! Penagok was the Penagok people's heartland. It was unconscionable, though not surprising, that the English would now seek to steal it from the Penagok. Waldron would became a thorn in the Penagok's side until Passaconaway's grandson, Kancamagus, and the war party he led did away with him a decade or so after Passaconaway's death.

Jonathan Danforth was one of three brothers who came to the Bay Colony from England. Thomas, Jonathan and their brother, Samuel had arrived with their father, Reverend Nicholas Danforth in 1634 from Suffolk, England and originally settled at Cambridge. Jonathan removed from Cambridge to Billerica in 1654 where he became one of the town's first selectmen, holding the office twenty-one years. He was also a famous mathematician but was foremost a surveyor. His surveying operations took him all through the Morôdemak River valley, as far as Franklin, where the Morôdemak was born out of the Bemijijoasek and Wiwninibesaki rivers. Jonathan would die in 1712 at the age of 85. Prior to his appointment to survey the land at Naticook in response to Passaconaway's petition, Jonathan Danforth had been sent to locate 800 acres of land in response to a petition from Billerica. He performed the survey, which included the land which he now was to survey for the chief.

Less than a month had passed since the Great Chief had received word that an important Englishman, the brother of a chief at Boston, was coming to survey land in response to Passaconaway's request. He hadn't understand the word "survey" but figured it must be another English trick to drag out an agreement over land.

Danforth and Parker, after an hour or so of conversation, set out to survey the land while Passaconaway, along with Standing Birch and Running Moose, got in their canoe and headed upriver toward Namaskik.

"He looks to be older than the mountains," Parker said, as he set up equipment to begin surveying.

"I heard it said that he is over 110 years old," Danforth responded, struggling with a piece of equipment. "I've never met a man who had suffered so much and yet bore himself with such dignity. It's hard to believe he is, as some claim, a great witch," Danforth added.

It took several days to finish the surveying. During that time Danforth thought more about the chief and how pitiable the situation was for him. He had never liked what had happened to the Indians or how they had been treated. He especially didn't like that the old chief was having to beg for land that should have actually been his anyway.

"I am going to include the two islands," he declared to Parker.

Parker agreed. As a result, in addition to the one and a half miles wide and three miles long rich intervale land that extended on both sides of the Morôdemak River, the surveyors suggested giving Passaconaway the two islands. Eventually, a year after his initial request for land, the Great Chief's petition was granted and the islands were included. The grant stated:

> "The order of the upon is as follows, Viz: In answer to the petition of Papisseconneway, this Court Judgeth it meete to grant said Papisseconneway and his men or associates about Naticot, above Mr. Brenton's lands (Litchfield) where it is free, a mile and a half on either side Merrimack River in breadth, three miles on either side in length provided he nor they do not alienate any part of this grant without leave and license from this Court first obtained."

A Petition for Land

"According to order of Honerd General Court, there is laid out unto the Indians, Passaconaway and his associates, the inhabitants of Naticott, Three miles square, or so much (eather) as containes it in the fiture of a Romboides upon Merrimack River; beginning at the head of Mr. Brenton's lands of Naticott, on the east side of the River, and then it jointh to his line, which line runs halfe a point North West of the East, it lyeth one mile and one half wide on side of ye River and somewhat better, and runnes three miles up the River, the northern line on the east side of ther River is bounded by a brook, called by the Indians Suskayquetuck (Great Cohos Brook) right against the falls in the River called Pokechous, the line on both sides of the River are parallels; the side line of the east side of the River runs halfe a point eastward of the NNE and the side line of the west side of the River runs Northeast by North all of which is sufficiently bounded and marked with an I, also there is two small islands in the River, part of which the lower and line crosses. One of them Papiesseconneway had lived upon and planted a long time, a small patch of Intervale land on the west side of the River adjacent and a little below ye islands, by estimation about 40 acres which jointh their land to Souhegan River, which the Indians have planted (much of it) a long time and considering that there is very little good land in that which is now laid out to them the Indians do earnestly request this Honerd Court to grant these two small islands and ye patch of Intervale as it is bounded by the hills."

Laid out by Parker and Danforth, Surveyors, 27, 3rd Mo. 1663

It was with no small surprise that Passaconaway received the news of the land grant. Islands were a favored site for the Penagok.

During the heat of summer islands were a cool place to be. Additionally, the breeze coming off the river blew the away the swarms of mosquitoes that haunted the banks of the rivers. It was a surprise that the English would give up such favored sites as islands. Passaconaway was also surprised, no doubt, that the General Court ordered him to pay the bill for surveying the grant! He would have not been surprised; however, to learn that after his death, the whole tract of land reverted to the government, and was granted in 1729 to John Richardson, Joseph Blanchard and others.

8

The Rum Incident

(1668 C.E.)

The story is set in 1668. Penagok, the "Place of the Falling Bank," now Concord, NH, is the stronghold and heartland of the Penagok peoples. In May 1659 Richard Waldron and Peter Coffin, among others, petition for a plantation at Penagok. During the same year the Penagok Chief Babiwseso-Ogawinno-Passaconaway, invited Waldron and Coffin to visit him while he was at Penagok. In 1663 the Massachusetts General Court granted Penagok to Salem men but they were unable to occupy the site. In 1668 two Indians were sent to Piscataqua by trading post operator Thomas Paine and his assistant Dickinson to obtain cloth, powder and shot in exchange for furs. Instead Waldron who possessed the goods and Coffin who held the license, sent rum and cloth. When the cloth and rum arrived at Penagok at least 100 Penagok got drunk for the night, all leaving the trading post except one who killed Dickinson while Paine was at the nearby Penagok fort. The next day the Indian who killed Dickinson was put to death by the Penagok. In 1676 Waldron organized a sham fight in which he tricked about 400 Indians, setting 200 at liberty and the remainder, whom he accused of atrocities, were sold into slavery and 7 or 8 put to death. Among those he had tricked was Penagok's Chief Kancamaugus, the grandson of Passaconaway. In 1689 Waldron was killed in retaliation for what Indians considered his breach of faith and friendship to them in 1676. From these facts, I offer the following interpretive account of the "Rum Incident."

"It has been 48 winters since they arrived. Then they said they came in peace!" came a biting voice.

Outside the palisade atop the bluffs overlooking the Deep Water the wind was calm and the towering high headed pine barely moved beneath a rafter's wings. Inside the council lodge the air was charged with helpless anger and resentment fanning the flames of battle.

"My father warned that this would happen! Now see what is afoot!" cried out White Hawk. Like his late father, Walking Bird, when White Hawk got his sharp talons and beak into an issue he would rip it apart as well as all who stood in his way. The only one who could ever stop them was Great Chief and Medôlinôwinno Babiwseso-Ogawinno - the Very-Little-One-of-He-Who-Likes-to-Sleep-So-Well. He was also known by his anglicized name, Passa-conaway – "Child of the Bear." Lately no one had heard from the revered one who had, it was claimed, lived to see 120 winters. Still, the Great Chief's admonition 8 winters before to "leave the English alone or be destroyed," echoed in every council member's heart at this meeting.

The elder who came from the small fort where the incident took place was anxious. His heart was breaking. The young man who killed the Englishman named Dickinson didn't even remember killing him. He knew this young man. He also knew the young man had done the deed. Or, rather, as everyone along the Deep Water who knew of the event felt, the rum killed both men. Now it was just a question of the physical fate of the young man whose body had carried out the rum's order and whose protective spirit had already left him.

"Skwedai-nepi has a mind of its own! It is maji! Very bad medicine that destroys a man's life!" came the ancient but spirited voice of Woman-of-the-Green-Valley.

The Rum Incident

Chief Tahanto nodded his head gravely in agreement.

One hundred feet below the bluff a birch bark canoe carrying the man whose fate the council members had gathered to deliberate on came to rest along the bank. The river flowed onward, lapping the sandy bank where the mica hued water curved nearly back on itself, reflecting not even the sky. Reflecting only itself. Before transporting the canoe below the palisade topped bluff, the river had already flowed over the white water and shallow falls, past the now notorious English trading post and the adjacent small Penagok fort and past the Great Chief's favorite island. The water was bewitching in its peacefulness, as if that was all it ever intended. Yet, everyone here knew stillness was not peace. Peace was often a time when enemies plotted with other enemies, smiling all the while at your face as they accused you of treachery on your own land. At least that seemed to be the new way of things on the land now that the English had arrived. Had not this very water carried the many diseases of the English that had regularly devastated the Penagok and their allies? Had not the river also borne the Englishmen who found the broad valley and who now coveted the ancestral lands for their own?

"The English will demand his death."

"Skwedai-nepi has its own power beyond our mind's control," said Red Pine.

"You must be careful with these people. Like their fire water they hide their treacherous side under a clear surface," warned Woman-of-the-Green-Valley.

"Why come out here?" asked Blue Sky.

"To take land," bit White Hawk.

LAND OF THE SHAPESHIFTER

Chief Tahanto looked deeply into the fire.

White Hawk continued:

"How can we allow a man to be put to death when he doesn't even recall the act he's being killed for? Everyone knows it was skwedai-nepi that killed that man! Nothing else! I have tasted fire water. It sets your brain on fire! You never remember what you did after its effect wear off." He shook his head in disgust.

"What happened has happened. We can't change it. But we have to be careful in undertaking our response. The English will be very upset," responded Woman-of-the-Green-Valley. "And we all know when they are upset they take it out on us not themselves."

"Of course! They set this whole thing up! That trading post is not interested in trade! Waldron and Coffin use it as a place of intrigue and deception. They use it to spy on us! It's worse than having a Mohawk fort in our midst! We only tolerate them because they are ruthless!," cried White Hawk.

"We should tear the post down!" growled Bear-that-Stands.

"Yes! The whole thing happened outside that post! Get rid of it," screeched White Hawk.

Chief Tahanto motioned for tempers to calm. He waited then said:

"This post was set up after a meeting with our Great Chief Babiwseso-Ogawinno and Major Waldron. We can not go against the Great Chief's agreement without our meeting with him and discussing it."

The Rum Incident

"But he hasn't been heard from for many winters," suggested White Hawk.

"He is alive, believe me! There would be a sign in the sky if he had died!," said Chief Tahanto.

"Besides, the Great Chief's son, Waolinasad, would never go against his father's wishes, either," said Woman-of-the-Green-Valley.

"But we asked for cloth, shot and powder! What did they send us in trade for our furs?! They sent us a handful of cloth and enough rum for everyone to loose control of themselves all day and night!," shouted Bear-that-Stands.

"Waldron and Coffin are bad men! They are tricky like raccoons and vicious like wolverines," added White Hawk.

"Yes, that may be, but Paine is a good man as was Dickinson. They too were tricked by Waldron and Coffin! Dickinson was killed because of a stupid quarrel over rum. We can't tear down the post because of Waldron and Coffin. Paine and Dickinson have always been good men," said Chief Tahanto.

"I feel Waldron is a man with a hidden plan. He does everything with purpose. In winters to come he will show his true nature. You will see," warned Woman-of-the-Green-Valley.

"Many will die because of him," she added.

"Yes," Chief Tahanto said. "Rum running is against the English laws. The English chiefs at Shawmut respect our Great Chief. They ordered their people not to give us rum. Yet, Waldron and Coffin sent it to us. I heard from the Great Chief Babiwseso-Ogawinno that some winters past Waldron and Coffin, among other men, had petitioned for their chiefs to give them our land while at the same time they had come here on this very spot and met with and accepted the friendship of our Great Chief."

"The Great Chief knew about this treachery?," asked White Hawk.

"Yes," said Chief Tahanto. "He wanted to look them in the eyes. He saw through their treachery but knew it was best to keep his enemies close. So, it seems to follow that the rum was a set up to get our land another way."

"One head two tongues. Like a timber rattler!," said Bear-that-Stands.

"If they want to fight, let's fight, I say!" shouted White Hawk.

"Stop shouting," said Woman-of-the-Green-Valley. "My ears are old and will break with anymore of your shouts!"

"Yes. I have to agree. We have been set up. They want this land. But we can't fight. We are not enough people now. If we don't order this man's death, the English will come and take the land," urged Woman-of -the-Green-Valley.

"What right do they have?" shouted Bear-that-Stands.

"None! None at all. They came here when my father was young. They claimed to be searching for the head-waters of the Deep Water. They went up the river and returned. Later we learned from our Great Chief that they claimed all the land from Wiwninibesaki south for themselves, including all our land," said White Hawk, shouting over another whose voice was not quick enough.

"True! When the Great Chief met with council after conferring about the English landing at Patuxet, the English claimed they

The Rum Incident

came for peace and to worship their God. But I say they want no peace and they are no men of good medicine! They only want our land and for us to die!," shouted Bear-that-Stands.

"I hate lies," agreed Red Pine. "I detest not being honest. This English man is dead because of not just rum but because of Waldron. He has laid a trap for us. But if we say this to the English, they will fight and we will lose everything. He is respected by the English chiefs. Now we must think our way out of it. The only way, it seems to me, is to condemn the man who killed the Englishman even if he wasn't in control of himself at the time. If we don't do it, the English will come and take over."

White Hawk shouted:

"My father said the English controlled fire and thunder. But now we also can. Yet we can't use it to protect ourselves. Each winter there are more English than fleas on an old bear skin. Now we have to use a gun to kill one of our own. There is no justice!"

Chief Tahanto sighed as he looked over at White Hawk seated across the fire from him:

"If the English come and take him they will chop his head off and put it on a pole. They will humiliate us. Then all Penagok and Abenaki brothers will fight the English. The Mohawk will then attack again. Babiwseso-Ogawinno is right. We must, at all costs to ourselves, maintain peace and friendship with the English so that we can keep our land! This land is our ancestral land. I'd rather live on it than be buried in it before my time."

"But a lie is death to the truth! Do you want to kill the truth? They are not friends! Is this the way of friends? Once you kill the truth you can't make it live again!" said White Hawk.

"The truth is susceptible to change. It shapeshifts. Our ancestors said that the only reality is that which is found in dreams. When we are awake we live in illusion. Who's to say that what we think of as truth is truth? It could be a lie. The only option we have is to live. Not just for us, but for our people. For the seven generations to come after us. He must die so our future can live," said Tahanto.

The consensus was that one would die for all to live.

As the council's verdict was carried out, Chief Tahanto looked outward beyond the pine trunks to where Windfall Mountain poked its head above the western hills.

Chief Tahanto hated rum. It had now killed his heart just as surely as he had to order the death of his friend's son.

The river flows on. Through all time, the Deep Water has flowed on, seeking its own level, even by dams, uninterrupted. Wearing away rocks, pushing sand and the stain of men's blood, the Morôdemak continues onward, unconcerned by mortals, choking in the human flood.

9
Disillusion

(1677 C.E.)

"They [the Penagok] were very near the English and yet though they were provoked by the English who burnt their wigwams and destroyed their dried fish, yet not one gun was fired at any Englishman." - Daniel Gookin 1675

Seated around the celestial council fire, the bear council members have an eagle's eye view of Waolinasad's entourage slowly making its way toward Canada along an ancient trail through what will one day be known as Crawford Notch. The entourage is led by the Great Chief of the Penagok Confederation, Waolinasad, son of the late Peacemaker, Medicine Man and Great Chief of the Penagok Confederation, Passaconaway. Looming above one side of the Ômanosek trail the massive flank of Webster Cliff scratches the cloudless sky; on the other side the brooding wedge of Mt. Willey casts a shadow across the narrow valley. The Ômanosek trail strides the boulder strewn gravel bed of the Saco River, called "Zawakwtegok" in Abenaki, and rises steeply as it threads north into the notch. From the top of the notch, the trail follows the Ômanosek River before meeting the Gwenitegw River.

As the entourage climbs ever higher in the notch, the temperature grows cooler. High above the despondent group of Penagok, Pawtucket and Wamesit early snow already frosts the peaks and crevices of Mts. Willey, Willard and Webster. Except for the muted green conifers and deciduous skeletons that rise into the blue bird feather sky, the gray brown jagged cliffs of Mt. Webster, and the tea colored Zawakwtegok, the riparian landscape is devoid of color. With the passing of the Leaf Falling Moon, Penibagos, it is now the Moon of the Freezing River, Mzatanoskas. Already the three hunters have felled Sky Bear; its life blood that had fallen from the stars and stained the mountains orange, red, yellow and purple, now lies lifeless and brown on the ground. Sky Bear has since been resurrected and has climbed back far above the trees.

As the bear council members, whose eyes flash as stars against the night sky situate themselves around the council fire, Fire Eyes, the bear story teller begins to relate a story from the life of Woalinasad, the Second Great Chief of the Penacook Confederation:

> Listen as I relate the story of Waolinasad's removal from Wickasaukee Island at Pawtucket (Lowell, MA) to the Penagok Confederation Capitol and stronghold at Penagok (Concord, NH) during the start of Metacom's War against the English. Listen as I relate how his trust in the English and their promises is eroded over time and how finally, disillusioned with the English and the promises made by the Governor and Council and broken by both settlers and the government, Waolinasad eventually heeds his wife's family's advice and leaves his beloved homeland for St. Francis so he can live in peace.
>
> Waolinasad had been aware, since 1674 that Metacom was preparing to make war with the English. Metacom had been attempting to enlist Morôdemak Valley Indians to join him. Waolinasad refused to join Metacom and instead took a stand for peace, removing himself and his people to Penagok where they would be far away from the conflict in Massachusetts.
>
> For their part, the English view all Indians in the same light; whether Indians be friendly or not, the English consider native peoples to be tricky savages and consorts of the devil who must be held under suspicion and if necessary

DISILLUSION

beat at their own game. The English relied upon the treaty that they had made with Passaconaway and Waolinasad in 1645 wherein the Great Chiefs had promised to be allies with the English. Therefore, when war broke out with Metacom, the treaty, as understood by the English, bound Waolinasad to come to the aid of their English ally. But of course, the English didn't trust that he would. They believed Waolinasad, whose people were closely tied through kinship and trade, would either take the side of Metacom or would try to remain neutral. The English would have to force his hand to choose the English.

At the time of Metacom's War the Penagok are a people who are beginning to split between those who want to continue to walk the path of peace with the English as laid out by Passaconaway, and followed by Waolinasad and those who want war. Those Penagok who want to fight the English are pressing Waolinasad's nephew, Kancamagus, to become their war chief and take on the land hungry settlers who have already eaten so much of Penacook land. Kancamagus, however, is not yet convinced that war is the answer. By 1689 Kancamagus' mind will be changed and he will become the English settlers' worse nightmare.

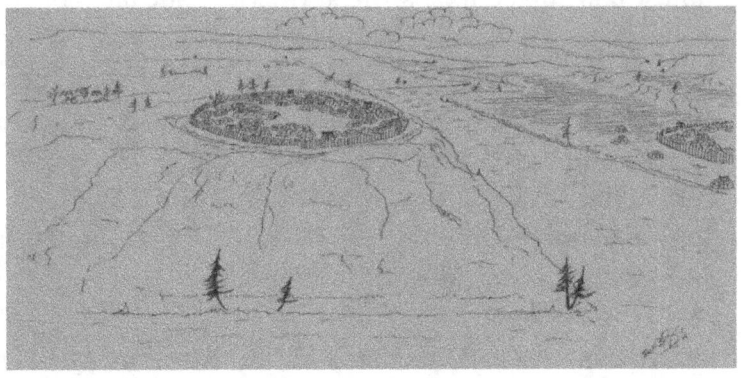

Sugar Ball Bluff palisade, Penagok [Concord, NH] circa 1675

Land of the Shapeshifter

It is October 1675; fifty-five winters have nearly passed since the English landed at Patuxet (Plymouth, MA). The autumn moon shines a ghostly glow over the Morôdemak River and the Penagok palisade situated atop Sugar Ball Bluff. The fort is empty. Further upriver, at Sewall's Island, Waolinasad sits with his council, pondering how best to proceed and whether or not to follow his wife's family's advice and head toward the French. Their deliberations are interrupted with word a messenger from the English has arrived.

Earlier the Great and General Court of Massachusetts had ordered Captain Thomas Brattle and Lieutenant Thomas Henchman to send runners to Waolinasad with a message that reads:

> "This our writing of safe conduct doth declare that the governor and council of Massachusetts do give you and every of you provided you exceed not six persons free liberty of coming unto and returning in safety from the House of Lieut. T. Henchman of Naamkeke and there to treat with Capt. Daniel Gookin and Mr. John Eliot whom you know and (whom) we will fully empower to treat and conclude with you upon such meet terms and articles of friendship, amity, and subjection as was formerly made and concluded between the English and old Passaconaway your father and his sons and people; and for this end we have sent these messengers to convey these unto to you and to bring your answer whom we desire you to treat kindly and speedily to dispatch them back to us with your answer. Dated in Boston 1st October 1675. Signed by order of the Council John L. Everett, Gov'r. Edward Rawson, Sec'y."

As the message is read and translated into Abenaki, many young warriors scoff at the promises made by the Governor and Council.

Disillusion

The elderly statesmen ponder the weight of the words before offering their advice.

"English words hold as much water as a leaking gourd," says a young warrior. "I say we stop hiding out and attack them and join with Metacom."

"We have never been 'subjects' of any one" says another warrior.

"You are the only leader we chose to follow, not the English" says the first warrior. "This land they say is theirs because you and your father made peace and agreed to ally with them. Now they say you gave up your authority by being their ally? This is a twisting of facts. It is an English ploy to take away our birthright to live on the land. The truth is that this not their land. This land has been with our people since the beginning. We have only allowed the English to share land not take it and keep us from it."

"Who says they have authority to give us leave and liberty? Only the Creator gave do this" says another.

"If you go to Naamkik (i.e. Namaskik - Manchester, NH) with only six men, the English will capture you" says an elder. "It is unwise to go there."

"I agree. It is a trick. A trick best ignored," says another elder.

"It is best to ally with the French. They will not take our land."

Waolinasad hears all the advice with calm reflection. In the end the Great Chief declines a response to the General Court.

The General Court, upon receiving no response from the Great Chief, determines that they must use force to bring Waolinasad back. The well-known Indian fighter, Captain Samuel Mosely and one hundred men are then ordered to Penagok to find Waolinasad and his followers and, if possible, disperse the Indian enemy claimed to be gathered there and "encourage" Waolinasad and his followers to return to Pawtucket. The Boston authorities also order Waldron to Penagok to help Captain Mosely find Waolinasad. When the English arrive in Penagok they find the Penagok Confederation capitol deserted. In response, as recorded by Daniel Gookin, the destruction of the food stores and wigwams was:

> "...a mistake for there was not above one hundred in all the Penagog and Namkig Indians whereof Wannalancit was chief when the English drew nigh (whereof he Wannalancit) had intelligence by scouts they left their fort and withdrew into the woods and swamps where they had advantage and opportunity enough in ambushment to have slain many of the English soldiers without any great hazard to themselves, and several of the young Indians inclined to it, but the Sachem Wannalancit by his authority and wisdom restrained his men and suffered not an Indian to appear or shoot a gun. They were very near the English and yet though they were provoked by the English who burnt their wigwams and destroyed their dried fish, yet not one gun was fired at any Englishman."

After the destruction, Waolinasad decides that for the safety of his people he will head further north toward Lake Wiwninibesaki.

At about this time the Wamesit Indians who lived below Pawtucket at Concord, Massachusetts and who acknowledged allegiance to Pawtucket and Penagok Confederation are wrongly accused of burning the hay of a Mr. Richardson. All the Wamesit men are arrested and taken to Boston where three are sold as slaves, the others set at liberty. Their liberty is short lived. By November 15th a barn is razed to the ground. Indians are alleged to have caused the barn burning. Men are sent to the accused Indians wigwams and

Disillusion

ordered out. Upon exiting the wigwam a Wamesit boy is killed and five Wamesit women wounded. This is the last straw for the Wamesit and all of them move north to join Waolinasad who they believe to still be at Penagok.

Upon learning the Wamesit are leaving Chelmsford the English order Lieutenant Henchman to persuade the Wamesit to return. An Indian named Weeoposit was sent to Penagok. By late November Weeoposit arrived at the Confederation Capitol. The Wamesit were still there, but were suffering from lack of food. Still, they refused to leave Penagok and return to Chelmsford. Through Simon Betogkow, an Indian preacher and teacher who had been trained by Rev. Eliot, they sent a letter to Lieut. Henchman. The letter read:

> "To Mr. Thomas Henchman, of Chelmsford: I: Numphow and John Line we send the messenger to you again with this answer; we cannot come home again; we go towards the French; our home we had help from the Council but that did not do us good, but we had wrong by the English. 2dly: The reason we went away from the English for when there was any harm done in Chelmsford they laid it to us and said we did it and we know ourselves we never did hard to the English, but we go away peacefully and quietly. 3dly: As to the Island we say there is no safety for us because many English be not good and maybe they come to us and kill us as in the other case. We are not sorry for what we leave behind, but we are sorry the English have driven us from our praying to God and from our teacher (Mr. Eliot). We did begin to understand a little praying to God. We thank humbly the Council; we remember our love to Mr. Henchman and Mr. James Richardson.: The mark of X John Line; the mark of X Numphow - their Rulers."

Land of the Shapeshifter

When these Wamesit reached Penagok, they found that Waolinasad had left. Eventually, due to hunger, the Wamesit return to Chelmsford. Major Gookin, Major Williard and Mr. Eliot are sent to comfort them; however, the comfort doesn't last long. On February 5, 1676 the Wamesit petition to leave Chelmsford for fear that they would be harmed. They fled again towards Penagok, leaving five or six behind in a wigwam who are too lame and blind. The Chelmsford people, again believing mischief is afoot, burn the wigwam and all inside perish in the fire.

The Wamesit find Waolinasad at Penagok but by then Mystic George and Sagamore Numphow (Nobhow), husband of Bess, the daughter of Passaconaway, had died. The Wamesit and Penagok remain with Waolinsad until September 1676.

In September 1676 Waolinasad, hopeful that his people's neutrality during Metacom's War will be appreciated by the English and that they will understand his need to be neutral, submits himself to Major Waldron at Cocheco (Dover, NH). The English had other plans. Waldron tricks the Great Chief and the 400 Indians who he had invited to come with Waolinasad to Cocheco. At a mock battle arranged by Waldron Waolinasad soon realizes he has deluded himself by believing in English promises. He and the rest of the Penagok are stunned by the English breach of hospitality and friendship and do not forget Waldron's treachery where at the mock battle he arrested half of the 400 Indians brought by Waolinasad even though Waldron had requested their attendance to celebrate the end of war and promised hospitality to all of them. Half the Indians, considered "friendly" [Penagok and Wamesit] were released; the others were taken to Boston where 7 or 8 were hung until dead from a tree in the Common and the rest sold into slavery.

When Waolinasad returns to Chelmsford with other Indians he does so with hopes to finally live in peace on his island of Wickasaukee. Those hopes are crushed. He finds his island is planted

Disillusion

and taken over by settlers. Also the Mohawk, deadly enemy of the Penacook, shoot at Waolinasad's son. In March 1677 the Great Chief's return is communicated to the Governor and Council by a letter from Mr. James Parker:

> "To the Honored Governor and Council. This may inform your honors that Sagamore Wonalansit came this morning to inform me and then went to Mr. Tyng's to inform him that his son being on ye other side of Merrimack River, a hunting, and his daughter with him up the River over against Souhegan upon the 22nd of this instant he discovered 15 Indians on this side of the River which he supposed to be Mohawks by their speech. He called them; they answered, but he could not understand their speech and he having canou there in the River he went to fech his canou that they might not have anines of it; in the mene time they shot about thirty guns at him and he being frighted fled and came home to Nahamcook forthwith where their wigwams now stand." Rec'd 9 night 24 March 76-77."

Waolinasad stayed near Wickasaukee until September. Betrayed and heartbroken, the Great Chief finally gives in and agrees to follow the Indians who had come down from St. Francis, some of whom were related to his wife. Mr. Eliot wrote:

> "He was persuaded to come in again; but the English having plowed and sown all their lands they had but little corn to subsist by. A party of French Indians very lately fell upon this people being but few and unarmed and partly by persuasion and partly by force carried them away. The fact is Wanalansit saw his lands taken up and improved which the Legislature had granted him."

On September 19, 1677 Major Gookin, good friend of Waolinasad writes of the Penacook's leaving to St. Francis:

"First this man had but a weak company, not above eight men. Secondly, he lived at a dangerous frontier place for the Mohawks that were now in small parties watching opportunities to slay and captivate these Indians, had lately done mischiefs a few miles off. Thirdly he had but little corn to live on for the ensuing winter, for his land was improved by the English before he came in. Fourthly, the Indians that came from the French were his kindred and relations for one of them was his wife's brother; and his oldest son also lived with the French. Fifth, these Indians Informed him that the war was not yet at an end and that he would live better and with more safety among the Indians."

As Fire Eyes concludes his story the bear council members look down at the dispirited group slowly wending its way along the steep trail through Crawford Notch, many of the half starved entourage wheezing and shivering from the cold. Many are experiencing, like Waolinasad, post-traumatic stress disorder, the effects of which will follow them throughout their lives.

"Such is the shape of disillusion," comments council member Scorching Tail.

"Does Waolinasad ever return to Penagok or Wickasaukee?" asks council member Great Heart.

"Yes. He returns in 1685, but that is another story..."

10

Up in a Great Cloud of Fire

(1682 C.E.)

"That Sachem once to Dover came,
  From Pennacook, when eve was setting in;
With plumes his locks were dressed, his eyes shot flame,
  He struck his massy club with dreadful din,
  That oft had made the ranks of battle thin,
Around his copper neck terrific hung
  A tied-together, bear and catamount skin,
The curious fishbones o'er his bosom swung
And thrice the Sachem danced and thrice the Sachem sung.
"Strange man was he! 'Twas said, he oft pursued
  The sable bear, and slew him in his den,
That oft he howled through many a pathless wood,
  And many a tangled wild, and poisonous fen,
  That ne'er was trod by other mortal men.
The craggy ledge for rattle-snakes he sought,
  And choked them one by one, and then
O'ertook the tall gray moose, as quick as thought,
And the mountain cat he chased, and chasing caught.
"A wondrous sight! For o'er 'Siogee's ice,
  With brindled wolves all harnessed three and three,
High seated on a sledge, made in a trice,
  On Mount Agiocochook, of hickory,
  He lashed and reeled, and sung right jollily;
And once upon a car of flaming fire,
  The dreadful Indian shook with fear to see
The king of Pennacook, his chief, his sire,
Ride flaming up towards heaven, than any mountain higher!"

[From a mid-19th century poem entitled "The Winter Evening"]

Land of the Shapeshifter

At the Place of the Falling Bank. It was the time of the Greeting Moon in the year 1682. The Great Chief and Puritan dubbed "great witch" Babiwseso-Ogawinno has been dead for more than a dozen years. In less than a dozen years the Salem Witch Trials will take place.

On this day the sun's fire is barely visible as a smudge against the mica sky. It was one of those winter mornings when the cold is so deep that not even a breeze wants to move in the brutally frigid air. It was one of those mornings when smoke from wigwam fires rose as straight as a white pine's trunk into the sky before gradually dissipating into the atmosphere. No one with a right mind was out and about on a day such as this. It was a day for story telling.

Sitting inside a cocoon-like wigwam in front of a crackling fire located beneath the roof smoke hole is Little Spruce, his father Talks-to-Moose, his mother Mountain Breeze, younger sister Dragonfly, and grandfather, Gray Bear. The wigwam is nearly swallowed by the snow banked against its exterior birch bark walls. As Gray Bear takes a long draught from his pipe, Little Spruce and Dragonfly ask their grandfather to tell them of the Great Chief's ascent into the sky.

"Tell us again about the Great Chief Babiwseso-Ogawinno!" asks Little Spruce.

"Yes, tell us how the Great Chief entered Wli-na-di-a-lib-na!" Dragonfly exclaims, her face eager.

Little Spruce and Dragonfly heard the story many times, as had all Penagok children during these more than twelve winters since the Great Chief's passing into the above land. All Penagok had heard of the Very-Little-One-of-He-Who-Like's-to-Sleep-So-Well's request to the Great Spirit that he be allowed to attend the Great

Up in a Great Cloud of Fire

Council in the Happy Hunting Grounds. All Penagok had heard that the request had been granted by the Great Spirit Gchi Nwaskw who from time to time descended from the above land and alighted atop Agiocochook when he visited earth. Agiocochook, which in another one hundred years or so would be renamed Mt. Washington after the first American president, was chief among the White Mountains. The White Mountains was sacred land. The Penagok, the Bemijijoasek, the Wiwninibesaki and others had long hunted and trapped in the notches and dales, but dared not go above the tree line where the spirits lived. Only those people who worked with medicine, the Medôlinôwinnoak, ever went there to commune with the Great Spirit. The greatest of these Medôlinôwinno-ak was the Great Chief Babiwseso-Ogawinno.

The Great Chief's name meant "the Very-Little-One-of-He-Who-Like's-to-Sleep-So-Well." His name was anglicized "Passaconaway" by the English who, perhaps, found the Great Chief's name too difficult to pronounce. Even Babiwseso-Ogawinno succumbed to the change in his name, using it and variants of it in official documents to Boston. It was said by the Penagok that although the Great Spirit revealed himself to Medôlinôwinno-ak Babiwseso-Ogawinno was the Great Spirit's favorite and that because the Great Chief was the Great Spirit's favorite, Babiwseso-Ogawinno was allowed to commune with the Great Spirit while dreaming and awake. When the Great Chief died, the Penagok believe, he left the world on a toboggan driven by a team of two dozen gigantic wolves up the slopes of Agiocochook and from there Babiwseso-Ogawinno was swept up into the sky in a cloud of fire and entered the Great Council at Wlinadialibna – the Happy Hunting Grounds.

"Our Great Chief?" asks Gray Bear. "I think I've forgotten that story," he teases, his eyes twinkling in the dancing flames.

"Tell us, tell us," Little Spruce pleads, his face glistening from the bear's grease smudged on his oak leaf tinctured face.

Land of the Shapeshifter

"Hmm... let me see. Well, the story...." Gray Bear begins. He then pauses to measure the effect his words have on his grandchildren. Little Spruce sits transfixed, waiting for the next words. Gray Bear, sensing his grandson's eagerness continues:

"As you know, the Great Chief was one of the greatest Medôlinôwinno. The Great Chief had been given the power by the Great Spirit to shift the shape of the elements. With this power the Great Chief could turn ice into water in the middle of a blizzard and he could turn water into ice during the middle of a hot and humid day. He was able to handle the deadly timber rattlesnakes which merely curled up and went to sleep in his hands."

Little Spruce and Dragonfly sat mesmerized by the story while Mountain Breeze and Talks-to-Moose looked on at them, shaking their heads in agreement of the facts. All Penagok knew the truth of the Great Chief's powers. Even the English knew and feared the Great Chief. He could change water and tame rattlesnakes and could do much more.

"It had been almost fifty winters since the English arrived in our lands to live. The Great Chief at first had wanted to destroy the English but the Great Spirit would not let him. The Great Spirit spoke in the Great Chief's ear and told him:

'Leave them in peace. It is my wish that they have come here. Let them be in peace or I will destroy you.'

"The Great Chief knew he could not disobey the Great Spirit. From the time the white men came to live in our lands until the day the Great Chief died he kept his promise to the Great Spirit. The Great Spirit, in turn, never forgot the Great Chief."

Up in a Great Cloud of Fire

Gray Bear became silent. The fire that snapped and popped like popcorn was the only sound that could be heard inside or outside the wigwam. Gray Bear continued:

"Now then, the day the Great Chief left us was in the middle of summer. It had been hot and humid and the white pine trees were sticky with sweat. On this day that the Great Spirit acceded to the Great Chief's wish to join the Great Council that was being brought together by the Great Spirit. In order to join the Great Council; however, the body of the Great Chief had to leave his people forever. The people were all very sad. You see, the Great Chief had been old when even our great-grandparents were young. He had lived for more than five generations of our people. The people felt the Great Chief would endure longer than even the ancient white pines. In truth we all felt as though we were losing our protector. The Great Chief urged us to remain at peace and to follow his son, Waolinasad, who had promised to follow the path of peace."

"'Remember,' the Great Chief urged, 'follow the path of peace. If you take up your arrows and tomahawks against the English you will be destroyed. Follow the path of peace,' he urged."

"As the Great Chief spoke to us, summer suddenly became winter. Then the Great Chief requested that a great toboggan be made for him. What he asked was done. After the toboggan was prepared a great cloud of fire appeared. It had been sent down by the Great Spirit. Out of the fiery cloud appeared twenty four gigantic white wolves."

"'Don't be afraid,' the Great Chief urged. 'Hitch them to the sleds. They will take me to the Great Council fire.'"

"The twenty-four wolves were then attached to the sled. The Great Chief, wrapped in his bearskin robe with a bear claw necklace around his neck, mounted the sled. 'Gchi wlwni,' he said, thanking us. 'Wli nanawalmezi' – 'Take care of youself' he said as the toboggan began to climb into the cloud. The wolves sped up into the sky, flying above the Morôdemak, over the quick frozen Wiwninibesaki and up toward the White Mountains. As they flew into the sky the Great Chief screamed with joy. He was young again! As we looked to where the Great Chief went we saw in the furthest reach of our eye's vision bone white Agiocochook suddenly standing out boldly against the backdrop of a blue jay feather sky. We saw the Great Chief driven up the slopes of the Hidden One by the team of two dozen wolves pulling him on the toboggan soar into the sky above Agiocochook. As it rose above Agiocochook the toboggan burst into flames and the Great Chief ascended into the above land."

Dragonfly and Little Spruce sat silently, envisioning the Great Chief climbing into the clouds.

"The Great Chief was always generous and caring," Butterfly said.

"Yes," agreed her husband, Talks-to-Moose. "He was very generous and caring toward all people. Although the English trespassed on our lands and then would not allow us to hunt or fish there any more, the Great Chief never advocated war against them. He never captured or killed any of the English and yet the English captured his son and wife and killed his people. The Great Chief acted as a friend to the English and yet they acted as an enemy to him."

Gray Bear added:

"After Waolinasad became chief, the Great Chief went to live on his island south of Namaskik. He had to beg from the English for permission to live on his own land! I believe he died with a heavy heart."

Up in a Great Cloud of Fire

"A very heavy heart" agreed Mountain Breeze.

Outside the wind picked up. In the distance, beyond the frozen Morôdemak and Wiwninibesaki, the spirits howled atop Agiocochook.

****

York, Maine. President of the Province of Maine, Thomas Danforth and his younger brother, Jonathon who was the chief surveyor for the Massachusetts Bay Colony, are seated at a gate leg table in front of the keeping room's fireplace. Thomas, Jonathon and their brother, Samuel had arrived with their father, Reverend Nicholas Danforth in 1634 from Suffolk, England and originally settled at Cambridge. Their brother, Samuel, a Harvard graduate, had been invited in 1641 by Reverend Thomas Welde to join with Reverend John Eliot to become colleague pastor of the Roxbury Church. Samuel had accepted and after ordaining in 1650 served the Roxbury Congregation until his death.

"Passaconaway died about 12 years ago. His son, Wonalancet (Waolinasad), became chief in 1674. He has been pliant to our desires but I doubt this fellow Kancamagus who Eliot refers to as John Hawkins who may well succeed Wonalancet, will be as pliant," Thomas said. "He seems to possess a less amiable nature. Then again, the old witch Passaconaway was of a more conciliatory nature only because he feared we'd destroy his people."

"Truly?" asked Jonathon.

"Yes. I imagine the old Child of the Bear is now in hell with the rest of the witches," the dough faced Thomas answered.

Jonathon, who had personally met Passaconaway when he led the survey team that measured the Litchfield land that had been granted to the old chief before he died was sympathetic to Indians and didn't share his brother's sour attitude toward the "heathens." Jonathon advocated peaceful relations and lawful acquisition of land not the skillful maneuvering around the truth when agreeing to "rent" land.

"I had heard that he had become a Christian" Jonathon ventured.

"Christian? I should think not," Thomas laughed. "I suppose Reverend Eliot believes he converted the old witch. Passaconaway may have thought he was a Christian but I doubt the veracity of the claims. At most Passaconaway realized it was useful to be Christian. He was a very politic man. It's well to be remembered about these heathens that what they voice by the mouth isn't necessarily echoed in their heart and soul."

"You doubt Reverend Eliot's appraisal then?"

"I don't doubt the good Reverend's appraisal that he believed Passaconaway said he believed; what I doubt was Passaconaway's conversion."

"When I met with Wonalancet he told me that when Passaconaway died he was led by a team of gigantic wolves to the summit of Agiocochook where he was spirited to heaven in a fiery cloud," Jonathon said, adding fish oil to the smoking betty lamp that hung off the mantle.

Thomas laughed at the suggestion.

"I doubt anything of the sort. Certainly I believe that he descended into a fiery cloud to hell to be judged as all his people will be."

Thomas looked out his window toward the gray Atlantic swells. "No, Jonathon, I rather think, though, that our days of peace are coming to an end. Witch or not, Passaconaway did keep the peace even when he had opportunity to take another road."

"Well, I should think they have good reason to want war. It surprised me that Wonalancet kept the peace after that Dover fiasco in

Up in a Great Cloud of Fire

1676 when Waldron orchestrated that sham fight between Indians and then separated them."

Thomas interrupted:

"We had to do it. The good ones had to be separated from the bad."

"Yes. The good went free but the bad were either put to death or enslaved. That very action caused all Indians to distrust the word of the English. It's amazing to me that Major Waldron hasn't been killed, yet. When I saw Kanacamagus he nearly spat when someone mentioned Waldron," Jonathon said.

There was a long silence. Thomas realized the truth of what his brother said, but what was done was done. Thomas hadn't had a hand in putting together that affair. Even though Thomas hadn't approved of the plan it was a fait-accompli by the time he became aware of the incident.

Thomas stared into the fire and said:

"Passaconaway's son Wonalancet is growing old. Once the son is gone and the grandson, Kancamagus assumes the chieftainship I imagine our relations with the Penagok will be of another kind."

The fire cracked and popped, sending a cinder across the wide pine board floor. Jonathon moved his foot put out the fire and glanced over at his brother:

"It won't be as simple to put out the fire that will consume the land once Kancamagus is chief.

Within a few short years the relationship did change. In 1689 Dover was attacked. The leader of the attack was Kancamagus who believed the only way to deal with the English was through blood. Major Waldron and many other settlers paid with their own blood that day. War had come and the Great Chief Babiwseso-Ogawinno's peace was dead.

****

I often think about the Great Chief Babiwseso-Ogawinno. Sometimes when all is quiet in the midst of deep night, I, too, have speculated where Passaconaway went. It is during such times that I think that perhaps, just perhaps, when I traveled as a child through the rocky cliffs of the White Mountains and caught the whiff of a balsam bough's pungent redolence as it sweated beneath Day Traveler's advance that the Great Chief was there. Or when dew cobwebbed the grassy land on a late spring morning at my parents' house in Franklin, he might have been there. Maybe, too, my ears were captured by Babiwseso-Ogawinno's voice as the winter wind whipped wildly wet up the slopes of Concord's Heights when I was searching for the site of the Penacook palisade.

In reality, though, I know my mind is just running wild with romanticized imagery. Or delusions. Or... maybe the Great Chief is an internal companion to us, looking down from the sloped white light of Ursa Major where he dwells, pulled up there by the gigantic wolves who led him to the bears who are annually hunted, but with whom the Great Chief holds council, the stars their fires that will remain bright as long as humans fuel their imaginations. When I look up into the night sky I see the Great Chief there, twinkling brighter than the other stars around him. Perhaps he is waiting to once again shapeshift to bring peace to the world.

It is believed by some that Passaconaway's earthly remains were exhumed in 1821 on Carthagina Island in Bedford or Reed's Island in Litchfield. It is known that before he died Passaconaway petitioned for land and was magnanimously granted land at his beloved Natticook. Natticook is located near Pokechuous Falls (Goffs Falls) and Suskayquetuck (Great Cohas Brook).

A New York Times article in the 1980s related how Peter Woodbury of Bedford unearthed the skeletal remains of a gigantic man who had been buried alongside two other men. In 1822 the remains were sent to the Museum of Natural History in Paris for study. They have since disappeared. In 1984 New Hampshire Governor Sununu petitioned the French authorities for the remains to be returned to New Hampshire. They are still, presumably, in France. Yet others say he was buried on Sewall's Island in Concord.

Today, although there are statues to many of the descendants of the settlers who arrived after 1620, there is no statue in his homeland dedicated to the great chief. There is a statue to Hannah Dustin who, depending upon with whom you

Up in a Great Cloud of Fire

speak was either a heroine or a murderess of the Abenaki. The only statue of the Great Chief that I know of is located in the Edson cemetery in Lowell, Massachusetts.

New Hampshire; however, has recognized him in other ways. In the White Mountains there is a peak dedicated to him. Mount Passaconaway rises 4,060 feet. The peak is located near the Wonalancet Range and Kancamagus Highway, named for his son and grandson, respectively. Passaconaway's name is also the name of a camp and a lodge.

My true conjecture about Passaconaway's ultimate resting place is more realistic. When I look toward the sky I see him up there with all my relatives who have gone before me, his essence caught up in the air and the clouds, the lifeblood that we breathe. Once inside us the lifeblood becomes the plasma that feeds our hearts and minds, death coming only to those who do not metamorphisize anger into compassion before leaving life's trail and instead stagnate their hearts while alive, refusing to pump in fresh air that purifies their nature... nature whose heart is peace.

Land of the Shapeshifter

11

They Hang Medô-linô-winno-ak, Don't They?

(1692 C.E.)

Nwaskwomak are everywhere everything is part of Gchi Nwaskw - the Great Mystery. Gchi Nwaskw is without human form and is divine spirit. Nwaskwomak are physical manifestations of Gchi Nwaskw that can be felt but not seen. The people who communicated with these Nwaskwomak are Medôlinôwinnoak - "Persons of Medicine." The word comes from "medôlinô" meaning a person who is of medicine. The word medicine is singular. The word "winno" means a person who works with something; "winno" changes the description of the person singular into a person who "works" with medicines as in a person who works within a specific field of interest or specialty or more so as in occupation. By adding "-ak" at the end of the word, the whole word becomes descriptive plural instead of singular. Medôlinôwinnoak are respected for their powers and treated well by the Penagok. Their Great Chief Passaconaway (in Abenaki Babiwseso-Ogawinno) was also Medôlinôwinnoak, though he was referred to by the southern New England Algonquian term "Pauwau" as well as witch by Governor Winthrop of the Massachusetts Bay Colony.

It was late autumn of 1692 at the Place of the Falling Bank, later to be called, Concord, New Hampshire. In the land beneath the ancestral council fires that sparkled against the night's blackness it was a time when the air was crisp and tart and snapped against your skin like you were biting into a crab apple. Winter would come soon. The air was also filled with the tangy sweet scent of fallen oak, maple, birch, ash and beech leaves as well as the slightly astringent scent of orange pine needles that covered the ground.

There were four here, though they were not the only Penagok at the Place of the Falling Bank. Little Tree, Walking Bear, Standing

LAND OF THE SHAPESHIFTER

Pine and Dragonfly sat inside a wigwam gazing into the fire. Every once in a while when there was a lull in conversation and the snap snapping of fire against log was still, the chill wind along the river bank moving past the birch bark walls would bring with it the voices of others huddled around their fires. Standing Pine, known for his quiet and peaceful nature had long ago been named for the symbol of peace - the White Pine. His wife, Dragonfly, sat next to him by the fire. Their cousins, the short and runty Little Tree and the solidly formed Walking Bear whose opinions were just as unyielding, had just returned from the south outside Naumkeag (Salem, MA), from the land where the English had now lived for over sixty winters.

"These English are very strange," said Little Tree, pushing a log with a stick.

"The English do have very strange ways," agreed Walking Bear, sipping on maple syrup sweetened pine needle tea.

"Strange ways and strange things. For example before going to Naumkeag I had never seen the likes of some of the plants they grow. And they grow flowers that have no purpose. They like them because of the smell. Some say the flowers remind them of home," added Little Tree.

Standing Pine and Dragonfly listened intently, like it was an elder telling a story of how crow brought corn to the Penagok.

"They also have animals that look like skunks but which they treat like dogs. These animals have pointy ears and long tails and cry something like a crow" said Walking Bear.

"Do they spray?" asked Standing Pine.

"The English or the animal?" Walking Bear responded.

They Hang Medô-linô-winno-ak Don't They

Deep laughter resounded up the river.

"The animal!" responded Standing Pine.

"Yes, but their smell is not like a skunk" said Little Tree.

"Yes, skunks smell more like the English!" said Walking Bear.

Walking Bear added "They have fangs like a wolverine and claws like a hawk."

"The English also have something like maple syrup that is the color of Day Traveler and tastes very sweet," said Little Tree.

"Very strange people," agreed Dragonfly. She then said:

"I don't like going where the English live. It stinks and it's frightening. I feel they are places of bad medicine. The buildings are dark and gloomy with the tops of the tall longhouses stabbing the sky. One longhouse I saw looked like mountain peaks."

"Yes, and they are forbidden to enter like the peaks of mountains, too! I made that mistake once and was soundly beaten for it," said Little Tree.

Dragonfly said:

"I think the worst part is that there is no children's noise in the villages. Children look unhappy. They are not allowed to be happy. They are quiet and sullen like they eat too much unripe berries. They always dress like their parents and are wrapped in cloth even during the heat of the summer."

Land of the Shapeshifter

"It is unnatural. Children should be allowed to grow naturally," agreed Little Tree.

Standing Pine asked:

"The English hang Medôlinôwinnoak, don't they?"

Walking Bear responded: "I have heard that the English chiefs at Naumkeag and other places nearby have hung people because they communicated with spirits."

"Yes, it's true" answered Little Tree. "They say they are 'witch.'"

"Those hung are forbidden, I heard, to cry out or to sing their death song. What person would be denied the right to sing their death song to show the strength of their spirit to those who torture and kill them?" asked Walking Bear.

"And the English say we are cruel and inhuman for our ways of war," replied Standing Pine.

"What is 'witch'?" asked Dragonfly.

"From what I can make out it is like a Medôlinôwinno, said Little Tree. "The English kill them. One of the Massachusett who had followed their ways told me about it. He had met with a non-Massachusett man whose woman was from an island country far away to the south. The man said that his woman was accused of starting the whole madness because she told the English minister's daughter about magic. This man saw the bodies and heard that one woman had been hung because she was a witch. Now he is scared to follow their ways and has fled to the safety of the forests where I saw him."

They Hang Medô-linô-winno-ak Don't They

"Yes and I heard they crushed a man under stones because he wouldn't say yes or no," said Walking Bear.

"The minister is Medôlinôôwinno?" asked Dragon Fly.

"No. They are against the power of Medôlinôwinno. They say it is bad. Their Great Maker tells them that all who follow Nwaskwomak are bad. Those people who use magic, herbs and such things are now arrested and put away. Some will be hung. Maybe all."

"Why would they kill a Medôlinôwinno?" asked Dragonfly, puzzled.

"Why? It is because the English act without scruples!" Walking Bear said suddenly. "Maybe they are afraid. They seem to fear everything. They have no conscience or understanding of life. Even our enemies don't attack their own people. To do so is against nature. You would be defeating yourself. These English attack us and themselves. They attack the very people that give them access to Nwaskwomak. Their minds are twisted."

"I agree," said Little Tree. He added:

"They claim the 'witch' brought bad medicine and caused disease."

"Like the English have been doing to us since they first came here?" suggested Dragonfly.

"I don't know. It is a strange thing to our way of thinking."

"Very strange," replied Dragonfly.

"How did this Medôlinôwinno make bad medicine?" asked Standing Pine.

"I was told that she scared people with her spirit," said Little Tree.

"Yes, but they also worked with herbs just like our Medôlinôwinnoak. I've heard that some English women know about medôlinô and that they are now targeted by the authorities."

"Terrible. A Massachusett heard this?" asked Dragonfly.

"No. They heard it whispered about in Naumkeag."

"How could the medicine woman scare someone with her spirit?"

"Some children said they saw the woman's spirit leave her body in the form of a yellow bird and attack them."

"I've never heard of a spirit taking the form of a yellow bird," said Standing Pine. "Usually they come in dreams."

"Such dreams would be considered bad. They would call it witch riding. They say that when you can't wake up from a dream that a witch is holding you down."

"Nonsense. Everyone knows that dreams are reality. It is when you are awake that what you see is not real. Dreams give us direction. They help us to know who we are and our future" said Standing Pine.

"What do these women 'witch' look like?" asked Dragonfly.

"Some are old and sick, unable to walk well. Some are very dirty and tired looking. Some are like any other Englishwoman. I can not see anything to show they are Medôlinôwinno. But they say these women's spirits fly at night on sticks."

They Hang Medô-linô-winno-ak Don't They

"Fly on sticks? What about these women? What do they do to them before they are hung?" asked Dragonfly.

"I have heard from some of those who sympathize with the women and men who are also accused that they are kept in a dirty cave under a big long house. Inside the cave it is very dark and floods when there is a lot of rain. The chief's people tie the women and men to the stone walls with heavy metal ropes. Each person is kept separate in their own space surrounded by walls and metal doors. The space where each person is kept is very small, often no wider and taller than they are. Many die from the conditions."

"This is inhuman."

They all considered what they heard.

Finally Standing Pine said what the others had been thinking.

"Then this does not bode well for us" said Standing Pine.

"How do you mean?" asked Little Tree.

"It stands to reason that if they kill their Medôlinôwinnoak and their Medôlinôwinnoak are not different from our ways, how long can we last? Remember they used this word 'witch' before to describe our great chief Passaconaway who was able to change water into ice during the summer and ice into water during the winter? He was a great Medôlinôôwinno. It was because of him that we were protected for so long. They have forbidden Medôlinôôwinnoak to go to places of Nwaskwomak. Now what will become of us?"

The question lingered under the moon. Up there, where the bear Nwaskwomak live and where ancestors sing to their descendants' hearts, a star dripped a tear.

Land of the Shapeshifter

12

Family History's Lessons

(1902-Present Day)

"Hegel was right when he said that we learn from history that man can never learn anything from history." - George Bernard Shaw 1856-1950

The following interpretative story is about a Canadian French-Indian family who came to Penacook, New Hampshire to work in the mills during the later part of the 19th century following droughts and loss of work in Quebec.

The white pines along the field's verge strained the sun's first rays over the mist shrouded field. Here and there robins hopped about and pecked at the ground for worms, while high atop a spruce a blue jay screeched as a crow swooped past. Less than a mile beyond the fields was the Merrimack River. This part of Concord was named after the Penacook peoples who'd lived along the Merrimack River for thousands of years. Less than a mile down river was Sewall's Falls where people had lived for 8,000 years and where, during the early 17th century, the Great Chief Passaconaway lived on Sewell's Island in the Merrimack River during part of the year. Further down river, where the Merrimack crooked against the falling bank the Penacook palisade had been built and where during the early 17th century the Mohawk warriors had fought the Penacook defenders.

None of this history was known by Joseph and Celina Hall. To them this was their adopted land. To Joseph, who had come to the United States in 1882 from Ste-Narcisse, Quebec and Celina who came with her family from Vercheres, Quebec, between the years 1881 and 1882, they were French and to outsiders, they hoped only to be seen as American. For them, a Canadian-French couple in a land that could be protective and racist, it was a matter of survival. Even Joseph's father, Edmond, had changed the family name from Houle to Hall in order to appear more "American."

Celina, like her father, Moise and grandmother, Celeste, were medium complexioned and had raven black hair and dark eyes. A result, according to family history, of her paternal great-grandmother, Archange Petit, who it was claimed by her great-granddaughter, Mederise, was Mohawk. But to be Mohawk or from any other tribe was something that was hidden, sometimes passionately. It was bad enough to be a foreigner at a time when protectionism was so rife in America without being Indian too. It hadn't been easy being Native American or part-Native American in Canada, either. Because of this and other reasons, the 17th century Jesuit priests in Canada had replaced many Indian names with French ones and created fake family lineages that went straight back to France.

Yet, the family knew the truth. Joseph was part Native American, too, though of what tribe he didn't know. He was either Mohawk or Abenaki, but time had erased the tribe and thus his history. Many of their Canadian French émigré neighbors in Penacook and other mill towns were also of mixed blood. The well-to-do French families in Canada ensured that those who were not of pure stock knew so no matter how much they tried to hide it.

Joseph tipped his head back and gulped the last of his early morning tea out of a white ironstone mug. Sleep still in his eyes; he gazed out the window facing the field, running the palm of his hand over his face, smoothing out his moustache. Reaching into his vest pocket he fished out his pocket watch. Glancing at it he placed it back in his pocket, stooped down to put on his boots, saying to his wife, Marie-Celine:

Family History's Lessons

"Est-tu prêt à aller?" setting his mug clunking on the oak table.

She was nearly ready to go. Marie-Celine, was also known in perpetuity as Celina, and also as Olina, Selma and China thanks to census takers who had difficulty with non-English names, was busy readying their two day old baby, Valena. Marie-Celine looked up at her merry eyed, high cheek boned, dimpled, mustached husband.

"Oui."

Today Joseph and Celina were going to city hall in downtown Concord to register their daughter's birth. It was a big day and they both donned their best, Celina, in a plumed hat and tight waist dress; Joseph in his silk vest and wool suit coat. Joseph and Celina walked out to the street car stop and within a few minutes boarded the street car to Concord.

Aboard the street car Joseph and Celina conversed softly with each other in French about an upcoming visit of a relative from Montreal, glancing out the open window as they passed the outline of Sugar Ball Bluff rising above the Merrimack. The bluff was devoid after so many centuries of the Penacook palisade. There was also no other physical evidence that for thousands of years this valley had been home to people other than those who hated "newcomers."

"Why don't they learn English?" asked John, a tall blonde man who considered himself to be an American of German, British and Swedish ancestry to his brunette wife whose lineage stretched all the way back to the Mayflower.

"Why do we let these people in?" his wife, Margaret, responded, a sneer on her lips, adding "my family came on the Mayflower and ever since it seems we've been allowing more and more foreigners into this country."

The man shook his head in agreement. John and Margaret gave Joseph and Celina a look of contempt. Joseph, a short, dark haired ruddy complexioned man and his wife, Celina, who was holding their baby tight shrunk in embarrassment.

"Damn Canucks!" John said.

"Go home dirty French!" Margaret said under her breath, loud enough for Joseph and Celina to know it was them that they were commenting about. "You don't belong here!"

Margaret said to her husband:

"Why do we let these people in? There are too many foreigners. They are destroying America!"

Why indeed! Although born at Concord, both John and Margaret were unaware of the history of the area. Margaret was not only a Mayflower descendant, but was linked to the area through her grandmother's great grandmother. Her great grandmother was the grand daughter of Major Waldron whose trading post at Concord, then Penacook, was the center of an incident involving rum during the mid 17th century.

John was also unaware that one of his ancestors was also a Penacook Indian who had witnessed the execution of his friend for drinking too much rum and killing the English trader Dickinson. He was also related to Joseph who, although both didn't know it due to muddied history, were descended from the same Penacook ancestor who had defended his Penacook homeland from invading Mohawks.

Family History's Lessons

But Joseph and Celina were living in a protectionist time – a time of convenient conservatism and of looking back with pride to its Puritan past. America however had changed since the Industrial Revolution. Life was no longer rural but more and more urban. In 1882 Congress had passed the Chinese Exclusion Act which barred Chinese from immigrating to the United States. It was also a time that saw a huge influx of immigrants from southern and eastern Europe. Between 1840 and 1930 almost a million French Canadians had left Quebec to settle in New Hampshire, Vermont, Maine, Massachusetts and Rhode Island mill towns. These new immigrants were greeted by fear and anger. Some Americans felt that they would change the character of America. They feared that Protestant America was being overtaken by Catholics; the dregs of the world. Some Americans, even in small New England towns and cities like Concord, New Hampshire, became hostile, while others hid their prejudice beneath their smile.

In Concord, which had since the mid 18th century been a British, German, Scots-Irish, and since the mid-1800s, Scandinavian Protestant bastion, a large influx of Catholic Canadian French was unnerving. Rumors spread like wildfire about these people, with some worried about disease, filth and overcrowding. These new people were different, ate weird foods and spoke French. Not even proper French. They were largely poor, living in unsavory tenements and as a result were accused of increasing crime and of unspeakable customs. What they didn't understand was that the immigrants, represented by Joseph and Celina, were looking for the same thing. Life, liberty and the pursuit of happiness. In the face of prejudice, the only way to live was to survive and look to the future. It was what their Native ancestors had done and what Joseph and Celina also had done. With typical French-Indian panache, Joseph smiled at Margaret and John, raised his hat and said:

"Good day!" then under his breath he uttered: "Va donc pétaler dans les fleurs!" Perhaps they would buzz off. Celina smiled and shook her head in agreement. No one was going to tell him to leave. Joseph patted Valena's head.

"Mon petit."

As the streetcar passed the gleaming white statehouse, Joseph smiled to himself. This was a good place. His country. His home. A place for his daughter and grandchildren to be happy.

More than a hundred years have passed since Joseph and Celina went to Concord to register their daughter. Now their great-grandchildren, one of whom married a descendant of John and Margaret, are part of the great melting pot that join the chorus of voices clamoring for protectionism as a response, in part, to 9-11.

"I don't care. There are too many foreigners. They are destroying America," my cousin Joe says.

I sip my latte and let his words go in one ear and out the other. His words are the same words, though a hundred years have elapsed, since our great-grandparents Joseph and Margaret said them. I also know Joe well enough to know that nothing I say will change the chiseled-in- granite conviction of my cousin. He believes that America's cultural integrity and traditions are being ruined because of "the foreigners that are taking over America." In his mind our family's own melting pot history is nothing. To him there is no connection to what happened a hundred years ago, not to mention four hundred years ago. So, while he drones on about the detriment of foreigners to American culture and the need for tightened border security I muse that perhaps in another hundred years the descendants of the new immigrants and illegal aliens he complains so strongly about will also forget their own family's history and will join the voices in complaining about the next century's immigrant group. Yet I hope that maybe our descendants will learn from their family history and not only tolerate but welcome the diversity that makes us a stronger society where life, liberty and the pursuit of happiness are more than words.

Land of the Shapeshifter

GLOSSARY

Abenaki-English Glossary

Adelahigan	Barring-the-Way-Instrument - a weir
Agômeneki	Europeans, "Those From the Other Side"
Ahô	Yes
Alamikos	the Greeting Moon (January)
Alemamtaôzo	He pound in a stake
Alemidoo	She has flown away
Alnizedi	Eastern Hemlock
Alnôbak	"The People;" Abenaki
Alômkasad	Shaman, "One who Walks in the Earth"
Alômkik	Island where Molsem lives
Anikwses	Chipmunk
Aodowôgan	War
Askaskwi	Green
Asenikiwakw	Stone giants; the first people
Asokw	Cloud
Asokwak	Clouds
Awanigeeknageek	Europeans, "Who are these People"
Awasos	Bear
Awasosak	Bears
Awasosamkwôn	Ursus major, the Big Dipper, also called kwatsiz
Awasosewawa	Bear skin with fur
Awasosewimenahan	Bear Island in Lake Winnipesaukee
Awasosewizata	Bear blue berry, a high bush blue berry, huckleberry
Awasosibemi	Bear fat
Awasosimadagen	Bear skin

Land of the Shapeshifter

Awasosem Legwasiwinno	Bear-that-Dreams
Awani gia?	Who are you?
Azikanapo	It snows like foot wrappers
Babiwseso	He is very small; Child (Papoeis)
Babiwseso Ogawinno	Passaconaway - "Very-Little-One-of-He-Who-Likes-to- Sleep-so-Well" – i.e. "Child-of-the-Bear"
Badôgi	Thunderbird
Badôgiak	Thunderbirds
Bamadenika	Where many mountains are; mountain country
Basaakw	Red pine
Bawiala	Personal power to wish something on someone
Bemola	Giant bird man who dwells atop Mt. Washington - some say he dwells atop Mt. Kathadin in Maine; see Maji Nwaskw
Benôko/Benôkok	Downhill; a downslope
Benôkoi	A falling hill
Benôkoiak	Falling hill persons
Benôkoik	Falling hill person; a Penacook Indian
Benômkahla	Sand falls
Benijahlôg	A waterfall; where water falls
Bilowi basaakw	Jack pine tree
Bokwjimen	Little people who came from tree bark
Bôbenôdagwezo	It keeps dropping branches and leaves
Cicigwitegwasol	Narrow brooks

Glossary

Gchi Nwaskw	Great Spirit
Gchi Zôgamô	Great Chief
Gluskab	Abenaki cultural hero
Goa	White pine
Goanegok	Pine Tree Federation
Gwikweskas	Robin
Inglizmô	Englishman
Kaukout	Crow's caw
Kejegigi	Chickadee
Kikas	Field Planting Moon (May)
Kinnikinnick	Tobacco blend
Kokkhas	Great Snowy Owl
Kokokhas	I am sorry - said by Great Snowy Owl to Gluskab
Kôgwak	Porcupines
Ktakoswôdi	Milky Way; "Great Spirit Road"
Kwat	Birch bark container
Kwatsiz	Ursus Major, the Big Dipper, also called Awasosamkwôn
Maahlakws	Black, brown ash
Madjahando	Evil power
Magua	Mohawk; "Man Eaters"
Maji	Bad
Maji Nwaskw	Bad Spirit; see Bemola
Majigoiz	Bad Little One (nickname)
Managwôn	Rainbow
Mdawilhak	Loons

Land of the Shapeshifter

M'dikolin	Sorcerer
Medôlinôwinno	Person of Medicine; person who works with medicine
Medôlinôwinnoak	Persons of Medicine; people who work with medicine
Mekomwiso	Assistant to Gluskab who used a special bow
Mekwi	Red
Menigwan	Rainbow belts
Mesazeso; Msazeso	White Spruce (also Tajesso)
Mikoa Makwigid	Red Squirrel
Minôbowi	Violet
Mkazawi	Black
Molsem	Wolf; brother to Gluskab
Môlaskwa	Paper birch bark, striped bark
Moz	Moose
Mozak	Moose (plural)
Mozokas	Moose Hunting Moon (March)
Msawakwôlozin	Palisade
Mskak	Black Spruce
Mskask	Red Spruce
Mskwmagw	Salmon
Mzatanoskas	Freezing River Moon (November)
Mziwi	All my relations
Nawawas	The Creator; the One who Comes Among us
Naniponsat	Moon; "Night Traveler"
Nanomkiapoda	Snake who travels underground and causes the land to move
Nda	No
N'dadan	Father
Nebizonnebi	Medicine water (mineral spring)
Nikkshigas	Hoe Tilling Moon (June)

GLOSSARY

Nolka	Deer
Nolkak	Deer (plural)
Nonon	Mother
Nwaskw	Spirit; spirit protector
Nwaskwomak	Spirits; spirit protectors
Odamô	Tobacco
Odzihozo	"The one who makes himself from something"
Ogawinno	"The one who likes to sleep so much (respectful name of the Bear) Totem of the Abenaki bear clan
Olaman	Red hematite
Ototemon	Totem
ôtsôzig	A pass; notch (in the mountains)
Ozigwaôn	Arrowhead
Pakholigan	Drum
Pamgisgak	Sun; "Day Traveler"
Pebonkas	Winter Moon (December)
Penibagos	Leaf Falling Moon (October)
Piaôdagos	Bough Shedding Moon (February)
Pmola	Thunderbird
Pôbnôdageso	Tamarack (larix laricina); eastern larch. Tamarack sheds its needles every fall. Grows in swamps and upland soils. Flaky dark reddish gray bark. Pale green needles soft and short small cones. Needles turn a gold color before falling in autumn. Bark used as medicine - laxative,

LAND OF THE SHAPESHIFTER

                    skin ailments, rheumatism, poultices from inner bark used on sores, swells, headaches, sap chewed for indigestion

Sagamô	Chief; Sagamore
Sagaskôdakw	Ground Hemlock
Segôgwak	Skunks
Senikiwakw	Stone people
Senômoziimlases	Rock Maple Syrup
Sibategwizal	Side streams
Sigwankas	Spring Season Maker Moon; Sugar Maker Moon
Sisiwan	Rattle
Sizikwak	Rattlesnakes
Skamon	Corn; maïze
Skamonkas	Corn Harvest Moon (September)
Skog	Snake
Skogak	Snakes
Skw Sachem	Woman Chief
Skweda	Fire
Sogalikas	Sugar Maker Moon (April)
Spemki	Sky
Temaskikos	Berry Ripening Moon (July)
Temezôwas	Gathering Moon (August)
Waolinasad/Wanalansit/Wonalancet	
	"One-Who-Breathes-Well"
Wassanmôganihla	Northern Lights People
Wibgw	Grey
Wibegwigid Mikoa	Grey Squirrel
Wigwô	Wigwam

Glossary

Wigwôk	Wigwams
Wizôwi	Yellow
Wlibamkanni	Go in peace
Wlinadialibna	Happy Hunting Grounds
Wlôwi	Blue
Wôbamagwsiz	Shad
Wôbanakiak	People of the Dawn
Wôbi	White
Zedibego	Fir balsam
Zogelônidegwa	Pimples; blackheads "rain faced"

Native American Place Names in New England

Ômanosek	Ammonoosuc River (Fishing Place)
Adelahiganek	Weirs, NH (Barring-the-Way-Instrument)
Agiocochook	Mt. Washington (Place of the Great Storm Spirit)
Amariscoggin Place)	Androscoggin (Rock Shelter
Amerascoggin Place)	Androscoggin (Rock Shelter
Ameriscoggin Place)	Androscoggin (Rock Shelter
Annahooksett	Hooksett, NH (Place of the Beautiful Forest)
Asepihtegw	Ossippee River (River Alongside)
Bagôntegw	Contoocook River (Butternut River)
Bemiawassok	Pemigewasset River (Bemi - grease; awassok - bears - Bears Grease River)
Bemijijoasek/ Pemijoaswek	Pemigewasset River (Swift Current)

Place Names

Beskeodanak/P'skeodanak
                Franklin, NH (Branch of a river or Forked Beske; Settlement Odanak - i.e. Forked Settlement)
        NOTE: Conjecture - no proof it was ever called this name by Abenaki

Gawasiwajo/
Gôwizawajo   Mt. Kearsarge (Rough Mountain)
Gchi (Kchi) Senisizokw   Great Stone Face (possible Abenaki name for Old Man of the Mountains)

Gwenitegw   Connecticut River (Long River)
Gôdag Wajo/Gôdagwjo   Mt. Washington (Hidden Mountain)
Gôwizawajo   Mt. Kearsarge (Rough Mountain)

Kôdaakwajo   Mt. Washington (Hidden Mountain)
Ktsipontegok   Bellows Falls (Great Falls)

Massabeskik   Lake Massabesic (Large Lake)
Massasecum   Lake Massasecum (Great Narrow Lake)
Menonadenak   Mt. Monadnock (Stands Alone)
Molôdemak   Merrimack River (Deep Water)
Morôdemak   Merrimack River (Deep Water) Ancient Abenaki word

Nôwijoanek   Salmon Falls River (Long Rapids)
Namaskik   Manchester; (At the Fishing Place)
Naumkeag   Salem, MA

Passaguanik   Piscataquog River (Landing Place at the Sand Bar on the Fork of the

Land of the Shapeshifter

	river-Pass-bar, river bottom rising; agua-landing; Nik- fork of the river)
Patuxet	Plymouth, MA
Pawtucket	Lowell, MA
Penakok/Penagok/Benegôkok	Concord (At the Place of the Falling Bank)
P'enegokw	At the Falling Bank
Pennaquiauke	At the Crooked Place
Pesgatakwa	Piscataqua River (Dark River)
Senikok	Suncook (At the Rocks)
Seninebik	Sunapee (Stony Waters)
Shawmut	Boston, MA
Wajo	Mountain
Waumbek	Mt Washington (White Rocks)
Wôbiadenak	The White Mountains
Wawobadenik	The White Mountains
Wôwôbadenak	The White Mountains
Winnepiscogee	Lake Winnipesaukee (Land Around Lakes)
Winnepiseogee	Lake Winnipesaukee (Land Around Lakes)
Winnimsquam	Lake Winnisquam (Where the Salmon Waters Flow out; Winn - outlet)
Wiwinijoanek	Dover (Water Flows Around It)
Wiwninebesaki	Lake Winnipesaukee (Land Around Lakes)
Wôbanaki	Northern New England, Southern Quebec (Dawnland)
Zawakwtegok	Saco River
Zobagw	Atlantic Ocean

PLACE NAMES

About the Author

Stephen Berwick, a descendant of northern New England and Quebec's Native American peoples as well as French and English settlers, was born in Laconia, New Hampshire in 1962. In his life and work Stephen strives to open minds and hearts, believing as Buddha did that "In the sky, there is no distinction of east and west; people create distinctions out of their own minds and then believe them to be true." Stephen, who speaks Japanese, Mandarin Chinese, and French and is also conversant in Swedish, Indonesian and Thai, has traveled widely throughout Northeast and Southeast Asia. A practicing Buddhist since 1981, Stephen underwent ordination as a Buddhist monk in 1994. His preceptor, the Venerable Luang Po Chan Kusalo, one of Thailand's foremost theologians, consented to Stephen's ordination only after considerable persuasion, allowing him to become the first Westerner in 600 years to ordain at Chiangmai's Wat Chedi Luang, a temple famous as the former home of the Emerald Buddha. Upon returning to New Hampshire Stephen began publishing <u>Asia-Link Journal</u> with the goal of promoting cultural understanding, respect and peace. Stephen also wrote a biography about a Korean-American woman entitled "From Ch'ongnyangni to Northfield" which was published by the Korean Cultural Service as well as two biographies about Vietnamese refugees which were published as part of the anthology "Voices of the Vietnamese Boat People." Stephen has received a number of awards for his poetry and was named International Poet of Merit in 1995 by the International Poetry Association as well as nominated as the Association's 1995 Poet of the Year for his poem "Exile," a poem that embodies the spirit of America's immigrants. Stephen is currently writing a series of seven historical fiction books about the effects of European settlement on the Abenaki peoples of New Hampshire with the hope of promoting understanding of America's past as well as respect and peace amongst all peoples.

www.ingramcontent.com/pod-product-compliance
Lightning Source LLC
Chambersburg PA
CBHW052048070526
44584CB00017B/2109